Raising

Hope

*Do not
underestimate
the strength of
the human spirit!*

KIM PARKE

◆ FriesenPress

Suite 300 - 990 Fort St
Victoria, BC, V8V 3K2
Canada

www.friesenpress.com

Copyright © 2019 by Kim Parke
First Edition — 2019

I dedicate this book to my 3 now adult children, Alex, Hope, and Andrew, without the profound experience of birthing you all and knowing in my heart and soul how incredible your lives are and continue to be, this book would have no meaning.

Bless you all, bless you all with the beauty, abundance, and love this beautiful planet has to offer you!

ISBN
978-1-5255-5478-0 (Hardcover)
978-1-5255-5479-7 (Paperback)
978-1-5255-5480-3 (eBook)

1. BIOGRAPHY & AUTOBIOGRAPHY

Distributed to the trade by The Ingram Book Company

Dedication and Acknowledgment, December 2011

This book I dedicate to my three children. To Alexandria, I appreciate you being the first to guide me into the role as your mom. To Hope, who made this story possible, and to Andrew, the little boy who would show Hope the way.

Carol,
I know
You'll understand
the LOVE this
takes.
Love
Pam

CHAPTER 1

A Soul's Journey and Interference

On April 11, 1997, I went to my doctor after experiencing three full days of vomiting, and being unable to eat or drink anything. I thought it could be a possible appendix issue. After a quick examination of my abdominal area, my doctor asked where I was in my menstrual cycle. I told her that I had just completed a cycle about ten days earlier. She asked for a urine sample anyways, which I gave her, and it was then confirmed, right there in her office, that I was pregnant. I couldn't understand how I could have become pregnant. My marriage had not been in a good place for some time, and I told her this. My doctor wanted to admit me to the hospital to rehydrate me, but since I didn't want to leave my daughter Alexandria, I assured her that I would drink Gastrolyte to do that instead. I really just wanted to get home.

After another day of rest and drinking the Gastrolyte, I could feel my appetite increasing. I returned to work, still processing the news about the pregnancy. My husband and I weren't trying to get pregnant. Quite the opposite. It was quite a rough patch for us, and I had suggested, not for the first time, that we would benefit from some counselling. I had said the same thing after our daughter Alex was born, but the suggestion wasn't met with much enthusiasm. We both agreed about making appointments, but then never got to a single scheduled one.

Things gradually got better after that, but it followed a pattern: Things would get bad, and then counselling was agreed upon. It would be my job to find someone, which I would do, and then by the time the appointment date came, we didn't follow through. It was very frustrating, and just before this pregnancy, I had made up my mind to leave the marriage, with our daughter Alexandria, who was five at the time. So adding this new baby to the situation now was not great at all.

I firmly believe abortion is a choice, and I was not opposed to getting one, but instead I decided to stall the move until the new baby was born, hoping that perhaps our family situation could improve. I am surprised the doctor didn't mention abortion as an option to me that day in her office, especially after everything I had told her about my marriage—that I had been planning to leave with my daughter because it was so bad. It was poor judgement on her part. This is Canada in the twenty-first century, and women have certain rights.

The pregnancy continued, and I told my husband very clearly that our marriage required 100 percent work and effort from both of us, and that I was not convinced our marriage was stable enough to survive bringing in another child. Despite his assurances, I just wasn't as happy as he was about the pregnancy.

The pregnancy went forward with me feeling healthy, and I was back to my usual self in no time. After the first trimester ended, and I was well into the second, I felt I wasn't feeling the normal amount of fetal move-ment, though the baby's heartbeat was good. I brought this up at my next pre-natal checkup, and my doctor suggested I sit down for an entire hour each day and count the movements. As I took a hour lunch at work each day, I was already doing this, but I started paying extra attention. In my first pregnancy, I didn't have to be completely still to feel the baby move. If the baby wanted to move while I was standing or walking, it did just that. With this baby, it was really worrying, as I expressed to my doctor often. My doctor didn't investigate further in spite of my concern, and the ultra-sound on June 6, 1997 came back normal, giving an estimated gestation of seventeen weeks.

This nagging feeling that something was very different about this pregnancy continued. There were things that I physically couldn't do, like running for example. My body wouldn't allow it. During my first pregnancy, I had been very active. I had joined a pre-natal exercise class, each of which ended with a wonderful mediation. With this pregnancy, I was working full time and looking after another child, so there was little energy for anything else.

CHAPTER 2

What am I being prepared for?

Moving through the pregnancy, it was now late September 1997, and I was at a pre-natal appointment. I asked my doctor just how big she thought my baby might be. As she palpitated my belly, she estimated my baby to be around five pounds. I remember telling a work bud of mine how very different this pregnancy was from my first. She calmed my fears, saying that just like all people, all pregnancies are different. This made sense to me. Even though I wouldn't categorize my feelings as "fear" per se, it didn't stop me from feeling, everyday, that I was being prepared for something really big—so big that I couldn't even really put words to it.

At 6:20 a.m., on the October 30, 1997, I registered into the hospital after my water broke. It's interesting to note that the hospital wrote October 29, 1997 in their records. When my contractions first started, the babies heart rate showed deceleration on the fetal monitor, so a C-section was recommended. I didn't want to stress my baby in any way, so I agreed to this.

At 6:40 a.m., October thirtieth, my baby was delivered. It's a girl!

I didn't hear a cry...

Silence permeated the room as my baby was brought to my side so I could see her. She had ten fingers and ten toes; however, I could see that she was tiny, with no fat on her at all, except for her cheeks. She did not look like any newborn baby I had ever seen. All I could think of were the concerns I'd had about my baby during the pregnancy: the low movement, etc. I knew that a fetal assessment, usually done at seventeen-weeks gestation, would have given us a lot more information than the routine ultrasound had done.

After leaving the operating room, I was moved into the labour-recovery area, and my baby was taken to the neonatal intensive care unit, or NICU, for observation. I was told that my baby wasn't hooked up to anything to breathe, but because of her appearance, they wanted to run some tests. Even though the hospital considered her premature, at just over thirty-five weeks, she did not show any of the problem signs of the other premature babies that I saw. They just went with that because the ultrasound had indicated a due date of December second.

In the recovery area, a doctor with a strong South American accent came in to say that my baby had a cleft palate, and that they thought that there might be a syndrome present. I was in shock at this point and couldn't stop my body from trembling. He had charted her and kept saying that she was asymmetrical and that the genetics department had been contacted. Now this was really starting to concern me. This was, in no way, shape, or form, anything like the treatment I had received after my first baby had been born, now almost six years earlier. This was also a different hospital. I didn't know that, if your baby didn't look like a normal newborn, your subsequent treatment differed dramatically. I wrote everything down, because I felt they need to know just how different their treatment is of babies who are born different. I saw a phone on the table beside me, so I decided to call work and let them know I would not be in that day, and that my maternity leave would be starting sooner than planned.

I kept asking about my baby and when I could see her again. It must have been a couple of hours before I was taken to my room on the maternity ward. A social worker came in shortly after with a polaroid picture of my baby. I immediately asked to see her in person. They wheeled my bed into the room where they had her, and I burst into tears when I saw her. She was so tiny, yet not hooked up to any life support.

My baby had a bi-lateral cleft palate, and feeding her was the biggest challenge at that point—a much different experience than feeding my first, which I will describe shortly. I began expressing my milk, and once bottled, we started working on getting her to eat. It was slow. Feeding Hope four to six ounces of milk took one to two hours. I did this five times a day for the first six months of her life.

Before I was discharged from the hospital, five days later, I worked to accumulate a supply of breast milk, expressing it every four to five hours. When I left the hospital, without my tiny daughter who was still in need of special care, they had a supply of containers filled with breast milk with the name Hope written on them

Alexandria was in grade one at the time, and every day I took her to school and then went to the hospital to spend the day with Hope, expressing milk and learning about how I was going to feed her once she came home. After her first few attempts at feeding normally failed, a tube had been put down her throat and into her stomach. The milk was literally poured into it, by a nurse, after a syphon suction was created with a syringe. They told me that the occupational therapy team was working on a way for me to feed Hope at home. This sounds very disorganized, but that is how it was in those early days. I wasn't given any information, because everyone was learning at the same time. I thought, *This is a baby that needs to be fed.*

Occupational therapy came up with a type of bottle called a Haberman Feeder. It was designed by a mom in the United Kingdom, who designed it to feed her own baby. Working with this bottle to feed Hope was time consuming, and you had to be careful not to squeeze the bottle when she wasn't ready to swallow, or else she would choke. You kind of had to get into a rhythm with her swallow. I found I had to go by intuition a lot with Hope. I did a lot of research about different therapies I could use.

I also went to the genetics library at the Health Sciences Centre here in Winnipeg, after the doctors told me Hope's actual diagnosis was Wolf-Hirschhorn Syndrome, three weeks after her birth. I found a small paragraph in a genetics journal there, which said that only a small percentage of children with this syndrome reach their second birthday. Numerous organ malfunctions were reported in the heart and kidneys, though Hope's weren't showing any weaknesses yet. I decided to treat her like I would treat any child of mine.

Hope's eyes were very responsive from birth right on through. Everyone agreed that the genetics prognosis did not jive with the symptoms she was presenting with. All these findings gave us lots of hope, hence her name. Hope was bright, full of light, and many of the nurses commented that it was indeed a good sign. She also slept right through every single night, from nine at night to six in the morning. The days were hard, but I certainly couldn't complain about losing sleep with a newborn, like so many mothers did. Who knows? Maybe Hope knew I'd need my sleep, because the days *were* harder.

CHAPTER 3

Coming Home

Hope came home from the hospital on December 7, 1997, once she reached five pounds in weight. Feeding was going well, and I was comfortable feeding her with the new special bottle. Having Hope home was a relief, because going to the hospital every day was exhausting. On the weekends, I'd also bring her big sister Alex to see her. The five weeks she spent in the hospital was worthwhile though, as they did all kinds of tests. They did a full body ultrasound, and discovered that she was born without a gallbladder. They also learned, and were happy to tell me, that her brain was fully developed with well-formed sections. Her hearing and eyesight seemed very normal as well. Her eyes would light up brilliantly when she heard her sister's voice. I continued to speak to Hope as if she understood every word.

During those first few months, we quickly developed a routine, with me driving Alex to school and coming home to feed Hope, bathe her, give her a daily massage, and naps. The winter of 1998 was a mild one, so I recall being able to go out for lots of walks with Blackie, the best black Lab ever! I could feel my new life being formed, and it was indeed different. It was a blessing that I could get out often into the beautiful, sunny, mild wintery days. Looking back, that mild winter helped a lot with my mindset, because I could get out daily in the fresh air, and we did.

Our days consisted of doing the same things every day, with the feeding of Hope taking up most of the time each day. At five pounds, she was taking the required fluid requirements for that body weight (sixteen to twenty ounces of milk each day). She drank only breastmilk until she was four months old, when she started formula and solid foods. She quadrupled her birth weight to a full twelve pounds by her first birthday. Still pretty tiny. Since newborns are only expected to triple their birthweight, this was seen as a huge success. A huge part of Wolf-Hirschhorn syndrome is delayed growth and development due to missing genetic material, which profoundly affects how a child grows and develops.

CHAPTER 4

Emotions:

Easing into this very different kind of parenting sure was emotionally challenging. Those darn emotions kept creeping up. When Hope was still in the hospital, I started having bouts of anger. One morning, after I drove Alex to school, I popped back at home, realizing I had forgotten the lunch I had made to take with me to the hospital. I got into the car, ready to go, and popped the clutch as I gave it a lot of gas. This snapped the timing chain of my car. I got a nice $800 repair bill to show for that little outburst. Looking back at this moment, I highly recommend exercising to let out strong emotions in a less expensive way.

A pivotal point came when Hope was about four months old. I was given information for the North American support group for 4p syndrome, which is another name for Wolf-Hirschhorn syndrome. I mustered up the courage to contact them. They sent me a package of biographies of some other kids born this way. I saw the wheelchairs, and other medical devices, lists of operations, etc. I also joined a list serv email group for a short time, where families shared information, sometimes daily, about raising kids with this syndrome. I really tried to keep a good balance in my life, knowing that otherwise this would be all consuming.

A week or so after going over all the information they sent was the first time I really got upset, except for the outburst of tears when Hope was born. A downward spiral had begun that I seemed to have little control of. I had never been in a place where nothing mattered or seemed worthwhile. It was a horrible place. My anger about Hope's birth had now passed, but I was feeling resentment take over. Resentment was building for my mother-in-law. I know now how ridiculous it was to blame her for the shortcomings of her son. All families seem to have some issue they deal with, or fail to, and from what I have observed, most of those issues have more to do with lack of interdependent, healthy relationships than genetics.

One evening early in March, 1998, my husband and I were out on a respite evening at a movie theatre. I'm not even sure what was playing; I was just thrilled to be out of the house for probably the first time since Hope was born. When we were offered respite hours (four hours a week to start), I jumped at the opportunity. In any case, at the movies that night, I noticed something strange. I had taken off my winter coat, relaxed back in the chair, and crossed my arms in front of me. That's when I felt a large lump on the lower part of my right breast. I couldn't recall seeing anything that morning in the mirror. The next morning, I called my doctor and made an appointment to get it checked.

The lump was the size of a small egg. When I went to the doctor, she tried to extract fluid from it. This was not possible and a mammogram appointment was made for two weeks from then. I didn't waste my time informing my husband about this medical issue of mine. Judging by the way he generally supported me when I was sick, doing so would not have helped the situation at all. I asked for guidance from my higher power and absolutely refused to let anything in that would take my life away. I flat out refused. It was that simple. One day about a week later, after picking up Alex from school at the end of the day, I could feel something happening in my body. It was sort of a rumbling to the surface feeling. That's the best way to describe it. Deep inside my body and soul, I could feel something coming up.

I made Alex her usual after-school snack and asked her if it was okay the if I took a shower while she and Hope watched some TV. I felt like I needed a full spa day, but this was the next best thing and all I could manage without having to leave the house. When I got into the nice warm shower, the dam burst and oceans of tears spilled from my eyes. I visualized all the pain and heartbreak of the past four months being poured down the drain. I am not sure how long I was in the shower; all I know is that I was able to stay as long as I needed. I got out, got dressed, and my evening continued along. I didn't even think about the lump, giving it no attention whatsoever, and when I had a shower the next morning, it was gone. Nothing showed up in the mammogram appointment, a few days after that, either. My doctor was dumbfounded and confused as she checked it against the diagram she had drawn almost two weeks earlier. The lump had disappeared. I realised that I created my own healing in my mind, and my body had followed its directions, 100 percent. How did this happen? I believe that I did it with my mind, but I also feel that my spirit had a play in it. Either way, I refused to leave my girls, and now I didn't have to.

Later in the month, while on my way to see Hope's older sister receive a "Terrific Kids Award" at school, I slipped on the ice just outside my front step. Even though I tried to ignore the discomfort, wanting to be there to see the ceremony no matter what, by the time I got to Hope's grandparents to drop her off, I could tell there was something serious happening with my right leg. I had to miss the event and go to the hospital. I had broken my tibia. I felt so bad when Alex didn't see me in the audience, but she did understand when she saw the cast on my leg when I picked her up after school that day. For a full week, I was not allowed to put any weight on my right leg.

When Hope was four months old, other supports began to come through. This began in the form of a children's development counselor, who came to visit Hope once a month for an hour. Marlene was her name, and the monthly therapy meetings continued until Hope started kindergarten. This therapy used toys that matched developmental capabilities and such. Hope didn't seem to have much interest in toys at all. We couldn't even get a consistent reaction from her, in response to smiling, or singing, or talking to her. At first this made me sad, because my baby didn't respond to me, but as I came to understand her condition, I was able to be more accepting of her. Once again, through this process, the universe seemed to be opening up more and more. I could feel my life changing in so many ways, and becoming more accepting of those changes made the transition that much easier. I could feel myself being guided and was really trying to be 100 percent optimistic about Hope's future.

I came to a fork in the road, and I deliberately chose to take the path of acceptance, because it felt so much better in my body. I chose to embrace the situation wholeheartedly. Hope was truly an inspired little girl to have made it this far, and I loved her unconditionally. Thankfully, Hope's main doctor had a very good attitude about her future. He would say, "Let's see what she can do!" Everything was uncharted territory.

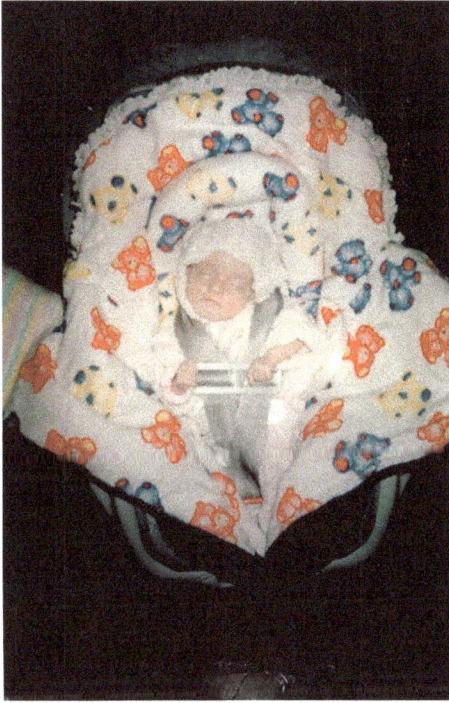

Hope when she came home from the hospital at 5 weeks of age.

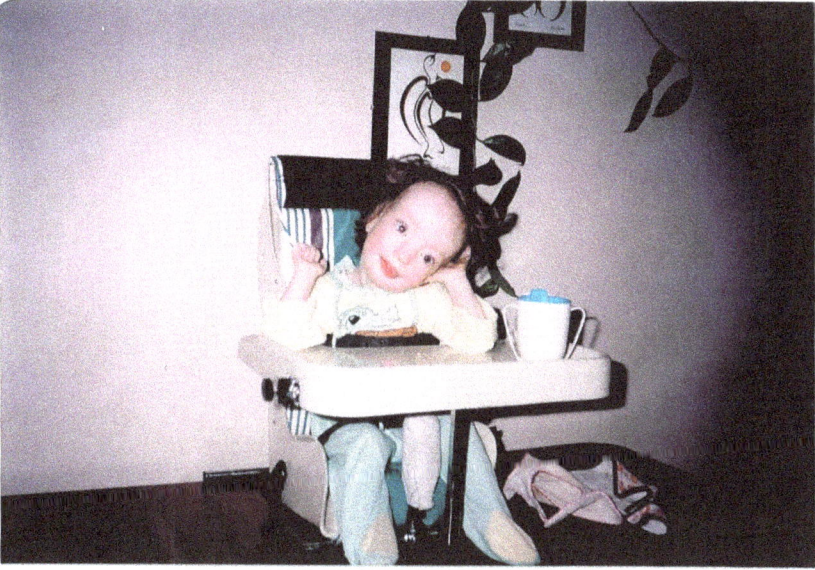

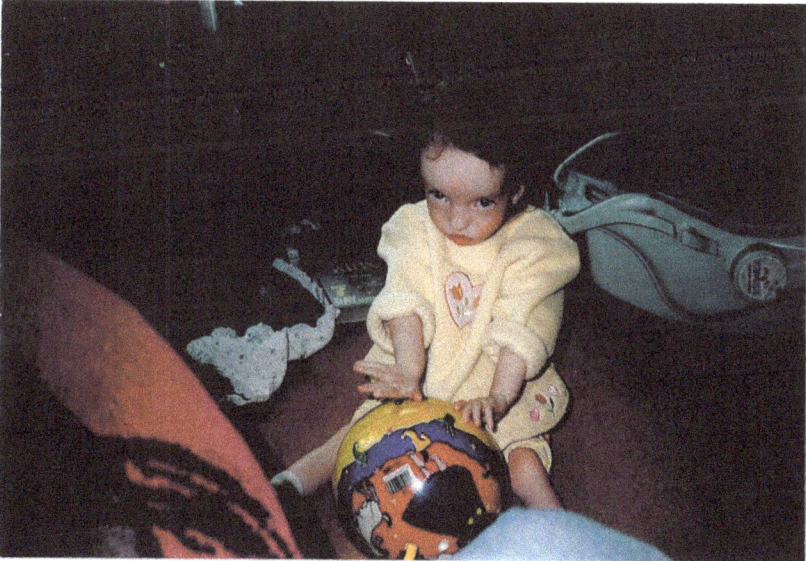

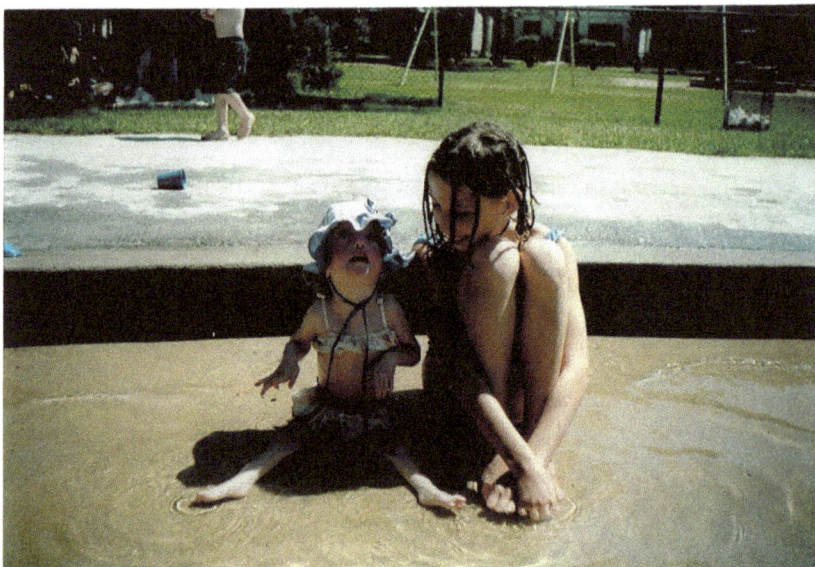

Hope and her sister Alex in the summer of 2000.

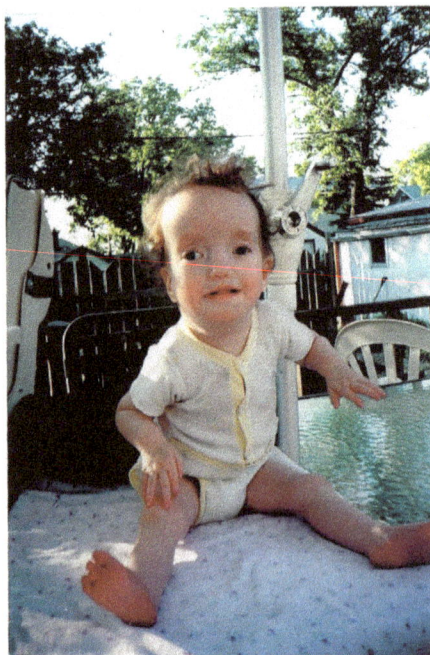

Summer of 1999, Hope can sit up and hold that position long enough for this picture.

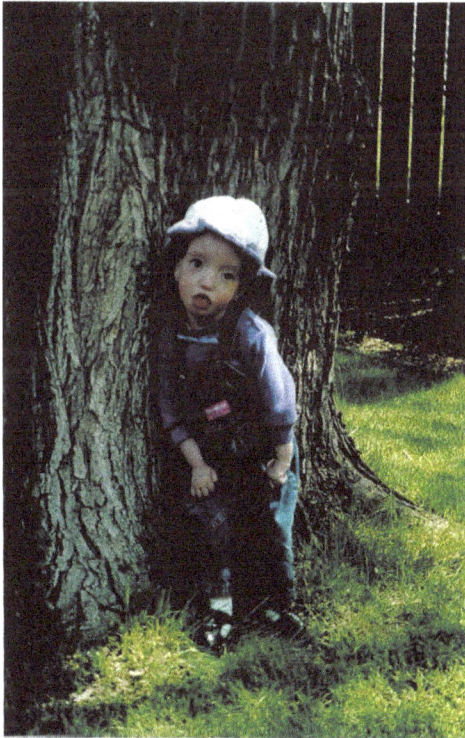

Hope is standing up leaning against a tree. She used a standing board for years, however she liked it better when she could lean against someone or something rather than being strapped onto a device. What ever works!

Hope at her christianing August 1999.

This is Hope receiving her most improved student award at her grade 6 graduation.

CHAPTER 5

Acceptance

So there I was, accepting as much as humanly possible, all the while knowing full well that there was really no known life expectancy for a child with my daughter's condition. It was February 1998 when I finally had the courage to contact the North American Support group for Wolf-Hirschhorn. I learned that there are groups all over the world, on every continent. When Hope was born, the genetics journal said that there were a hundred and twenty cases in the world. It was acceptance that really helped me process what had happened. I think that, if I hadn't had my experience with the lump, my negative feelings could have thrown me for more of a loop than they did. After the lump, it seemed like I knew just how bad it could get and was determined that I wasn't going to go there again. It was almost like the universe showed me just how bad things could get, so I would remember that I had lots to be grateful for. I learned to count my blessings, and I wanted very much to be a good example for Alex. If you cannot change something that has happened in your life, you can trust me when I say that you will find relief when you change the way you think about it. I am not saying I was happy with what had happened in my life. I would have traded anything for Hope to have been born normal; however, because that didn't happen and there was nothing I could do to change it, acceptance was the only way to move forward.

CHAPTER 6

Therapists

As I've said, Hope started to see a child development councillor at four months old, and her physical and occupational therapies kicked in at six and nine months old. I no longer had to take her to the hospital for these sessions, as the therapists came to the house. Progress was slow. Her main issues (aside from feeding) was hypotonia, which is a fancy word for low muscle tone. I would get a list of exercises to do with Hope in between therapy visits. I also taught these to Hope's other therapists, so that everyone could see what we were working on. The therapists would go to the daycare or wherever she happened to be. Even before Hope's first birthday, she could bear her body weight, though only for a split second. Even though it would take many more years for Hope to master walking, her neurological system was introduced early to the body sensations that would help her form a memory of upright walking.

At nine months of age, Hope had her first grand mal seizure. Eventually she was prescribed a rescue medication that she would be given sublingually; however, prior to that, those early years of seizures were a challenge. They all started from fevers due to ear infections, and would often lead to two or three-day hospital stays. In July 1998, we went to Minneapolis and met about fifty other families from across the USA, raising children with the same syndrome. It was an informative few days and very eye opening in terms of the range of difficulties these kids can have. It was a very organized group, had leading medical guests appearing, and offered workshops on various challenges these kids seem to have to face as they grow.

After that seizure in July 1998, I called an ambulance right away. She was transported to hospital, and spent many hours in resuscitation, because all the drugs they gave her to stop the seizure also stopped her breathing. Then she had to be intubated, so she spent twenty-four hours in intensive care. This process repeated itself at least half a dozen times before her second birthday. Then in April 2002, after two seizure-free years, Hope had a another one. Hope never had any lasting ill effects from these seizures though, and oddly enough, they actually woke her muscles up somehow.

At this time in our marriage, my husband and I were on our third attempt at getting counseling. We went to several sessions, and although we were both able to get some issues out in the open, not much was resolved and the sessions eventually came to an end. It takes two people to work on a marriage, and at our last session, the councillor said to me, "Well, it looks as though your husband is taking care of himself, so why don't you start taking care of yourself?"

I can certainly see the logic in this statement, and had always been a woman committed to self-care, so I started to use the respite hours just for myself and the children. I asked for and received some more hours, and in addition to getting Alex to her activities (as she was in Sparks and Brownies and synchronized swimming at that time), I used a good three to four hours a week for yoga or another exercise class for myself.

CHAPTER 7

Back to Work

I was expected back to work by July 1998, when Hope was nine months old. I took the additional three months unpaid. I checked with the only special-needs daycare the case worker said had an available spot. It was all the way across the city, and when I called to inquire, they said it was over $1200 a month. This would not work. Too costly, plus I had another child in daycare who was already $400 per moth. After discussing with Hope's father the possibility of his parents caring for her, we asked them and they agreed. It worked out very well, as they lived about five minutes from where I worked. I would go there at lunchtime and could schedule Hope's therapists to be there at the same time. This worked out nicely, and both Hope and her grandparents enjoyed spending so much time together. It did, however, become too much for them, as they were both in their late seventies at that time.

After Hope, I was sure I wasn't going to have any more kids. After Hope, her father wanted to try again, but I was not ready or willing at the time. As the years passed though, healing took place, and at thirty-six years old, after a long, good stretch of our marriage (the longest one yet), I communicated to my husband that I'd be open to discussing the possibility of another child. I was feeling that we were all settling into our unfortunate circumstance, and life goes on, so to speak. Then, when I got pregnant again, I had many people ask me if I wasn't afraid to try again. I replied, "Of course not! Why would I be?" It's amazing how others like to project their fears onto you. It was a fearful time of course. As I recall, the Y2K business was going on. It was Sept 9, 1999, and everyone was on edge, but I was just sailing through a great pregnancy, feeling good, and knowing full well that everything felt just wonderful with this new baby. It's interesting how in tune moms are with their pregnancies. Not once did I think anything would be going on with my baby that wasn't just how it should be.

Andrew was born May 18, 2000, and he was healthy.

I was sure about my decision to have him, because I wanted another baby and also a sibling whose normal development would be a great model for his big sister Hope. As babies, Hope and Andrew did everything together. It was tricky in the beginning, getting nursing established for him while meeting the needs of his two sisters. I spoke with Jackie, who was the case worker we had at the time, and asked for more help. I got sixteen more hours of respite, which was wonderful. This gave me a respite worker every morning, from eight until noon, who would come over and help out with Hope, getting her dressed and fed and ready for the day. Jackie was highly regarded in the system by every therapist that Hope had, and always addressed the needs of the whole family, and especially the child. In my world, that focus needs to be the number one priority for anyone entering such a career.

From May to September I had extra help during the week, and by September 2000, Andrew was well into his own routine. In the afternoon, I would take the kids to the park, or sometimes the beach. Alex would generally bring a friend to play with while I was with her younger siblings. It was really a fun summer, with plenty of warm summer days. Our respite worker moved to Brandon, and it was almost three months before someone else was found. Her name was Jenn, and she fit very nicely into our family. As Andrew was now older and more independent, I signed up for a Tai Chi class every Monday evening.

That summer, my husband was away a lot, "building a career." I had no issue supporting him in this, as I was at home now, and we had moved into a larger more comfortable home. Our first home was a clear title, so this was a good move for us. One Saturday morning in late September, my husband went out with his friend Scott, who had come over asking if Tony (my husband) would help him out at the dump. He said he would be home for our planned barbecue. I ended up eating with the kids and getting them to bed, except for Alex who was at a friend's house. There was no sign of him. No phone call or anything. It was almost nine o'clock when I got a call from my father-in-law, telling me that my husband had been picked up by the police for driving under the influence of alcohol and was spending the night in custody. Since there had already been a few other disrespectful events that summer, I told his father that he could come and pick up some of Tony's clothes, because he wasn't welcome to come back home to live with us. Enough was enough!

A few days later, my husband called to say that he had spoken to his work, telling them that he had lost his driver's licence. Then he had asked if he could come home. Since he had come forward with this work about his problem, and was taking steps to recover, I agreed to see how things would go. He had someone from work who agreed to pick him up in the mornings and drop him off after work everyday. He also agreed to keep his appointment with an addictions counselor. I told him that I would have to think about it, because I had heard this all before. He admitted that he had an issue with alcohol and that he needed help. And he made an appointment with the counselor, who told him that, if he could quit drinking for six weeks, he didn't have a drinking problem.

Just one day after the six weeks, he brought home a six-pack of beer. My heart sank when I heard the clanking of beer bottles as the case was placed on the floor next to the basement stairs. When I asked him about the counselor at AFM, he told me that he was okay now that he could go six weeks without a beer. We were right back where we started from, except that this was the first time he had acknowledged that there was a problem without a lot of anger and denial.

CHAPTER 8

Transitions

This would be the first Christmas in our new home. With Andrew being seven months old, it was a lot of fun, and when I look back at the photos taken then, the children looked very happy.

Early in 2001, we started to renovate the basement. Looking back, I am not sure if this was a priority or a distraction. I noticed we got sicker that winter. I was trying to get Hope back into the daycare in preparation for getting back to work full time. She just kept getting sick, but we did manage to slowly get her to a full five days a week (up from two days). This was a rough winter, and I could feel a low-level depression, which had been building ever since my husband's return to drinking. I was focusing all my energies on my self-care and on the children, and the big plan was to get back to work as soon as possible, no matter what. Our marriage wasn't showing much improvement after my husband's last string of empty promises.

Since my teens, my personnel passion had been practising de-stressing techniques, such as massages, facials, and spas. While exploring the up and coming spa and relaxation industry, I was introduced to a Reiki session in May 2001. Reiki is a style of Japanese alternative healing, in which universal energy is transferred to the patient via the practitioner's palms, a practice that promotes emotional and physical healing. After my first session, I felt incredibly grounded and capable. My stress was at an all-time high, and this came just in time to help me avoid having a total nervous breakdown.

There were so many things to get together in preparation for getting back to work. I think it would be appropriate here to tell you that my parents live in the same city as us, about ten minutes away. They joined the Jehovah Witnesses when I got married, and after that, we started spending less and less time together. They would visit once in a while when I invited them, but they never offered to help with anything. I looked for help that August and signed up for a family-awareness healing group that offered a ten-week course. It was after that course that I started back with Al-Anon. I still have the folder of all resources I found there, and here is one of the papers contained therein.

VS ADDICTED FAMILY SYSTEMS	Healthy	Addicted
Rules	• clear, consistent • discussed • negotiable	• unclear, contradictory • random, capricious Don't feel Don't trust Don't talk
Roles	• free movement between roles • facilitates growth • source of pride	• locked into one role • stunts development • source of shame Hero, Scapegoat Lost child, Mascot, Co-dependent, Addict Victim, Rescuer, etc.
Rituals	• regular, reliable, treasured	• non-existent or unpredictable • dreaded, associated with the addiction
Hierarchies	• parental responsibilities remain with parents • stability, security • freedom to be a child	• role reversal • role confusion • improper balance of family • power, financial and emotional • burden
Boundaries	• clear • autonomous • respected • flexible	• blurred • intrusive/enmeshed • violated • rigid/wide-open
Communication	• direct • clear • effective • self-esteem enhancing • overt	• indirect • unclear • ineffective • shaming • covert
Interactional Patterns	• emotional closeness • relaxed atmosphere • spontaneous • openness, moderation • mature, reflective • trusting own perceptions, interpretations, beliefs	• emotional distance • tense atmosphere • cautious • defensive, extreme • impulsive, out-of-control • mistrust of perceptions, interpretations, beliefs • questions what is normal

17

Obtained this handout after participating in an indepth supoort group at AFM called Family Awareness of Addictions in Manitoba.

CHAPTER 9

Taking Time to Heal

After my very first Reiki session in May 2001, I made an appointment to have another one. The release and relaxation were so amazing. I started to see the similarities of how my mom was when I was growing up and myself in my adult life. I can say that my grandmother on my mom's side is the only one in my family who gave me real love. My mom didn't seem to approve of that, and my hunch is that it had something to do with jealousy. Neither of my parents were able to give their children the emotional support they needed. People who have unmet needs regarding love in their families of origin become selfish as adults, unless they do something to heal this part of them. Many people did not get what they needed from their parents. Then there are those who got too much from them and became unbalanced in other ways. The truth is that I only felt love from my parents when I did something for them. So as a child, I craved love. This is the number one priority for children: being loved just for who there are, and not for what they can do for you.

In July 2001, I signed up to learn first-degree Reiki. It was interesting to learn about a new healing modality that I had never heard of before. I am glad I was introduced to it, as I was planning to get back to work and would need all the self-care tools I could use.

In September 2001, I started a family awareness program with AFM. Every Monday evening for ten weeks. Thank goodness for respite, because I couldn't rely on my husband to watch the kids while I attended this. Unraveling this mess of a life took a lot of work, and I had to be committed to healing. The result was priceless though. This program was helpful in identifying patterns of behaviour that play out in families dealing with addictions and the roles each person plays in those family systems. You cannot heal something that you refuse to shed a light on. Following this program, I returned to Al-Anon every Monday evening, got a sponsor right away, and started working very hard on the steps.

Taking care of my children and my commitment to healing from all this trauma was my priority, as I had completely let go of any control I had, or (more accurately) thought I had, over my husband and his actions. Even though at the time I felt that my marriage was coming to an end, my sponsor had suggested that members stay in the program for one full year before they make any decisions to end a relationship. I wasn't really a newcomer to Al-Anon. I started in Al-Anon in 1991, after my husband told me he would stop drinking if I got pregnant. My big lesson there was to never believe words from anyone; always look at their actions. People lie, including to themselves.

I often wonder why my husband was so intent on starting a family. Isn't it usually the women who have that biological clock ticking? It made me wonder, years later, if it was his mother who kept pressing him. She loved babies. Who doesn't love them? However, it's important that people have them for the right reasons. They are not puppy dogs that do everything you want them too. When my husband brought up the topic of starting a family, my response was always the same: "When I see an environment that is supportive of raising a family, for example without the beers pretty much every evening, I will consider it."

His reply? "I need a reason to change!" This led me to stop taking the pill. Maybe he was serious, as he was the one bringing it up all the time. Well, that's how I started in Al-Anon: pregnant and finding out just how powerless I was over alcohol. I didn't stay in the Al-Anon program after the baby was born—no doubt another mistake. I did learn a lot in that program though. Baby steps, as they say.

Having those years in Al-Anon sure did help in terms of my well being and interdependent relationships, both at home and at work. I could see common threads of the Al-Anon program woven into a lot of other self-improvement material I had been studying since my late teens. I unconsciously must have known my family of origin was not a good model to follow and had a thirst for that type of knowledge. My experience has shown me that anyone who comes into this sort of work has a background of dysfunction of some sort. Living with someone with addiction issues does affect the whole family, and it's important for everyone to get support through this.

When the children lived with me, I was involved with helping out an Alateen group (Al-Anon for teens). It helps when people all get help (even though they aren't the ones with the addiction), because often family members enable the addiction to continue for many reasons. Sometimes it's because they are afraid of change, or they are benefitting somehow from it. Either way, Al-Anon was a guiding force for me during this difficult time. All the members there are different, but their stories are quite the same. It is a spiritual program based on the twelve steps, where you reach your own conclusions about your life, while healing and regaining your strength, gaining confidence by good self-care, and letting go of what the addicted person does. The main point there is that you learn to let go, with love.

Heading back to work was a real challenge. It seemed (and I can only say this looking back at those years) that my husband's addiction grew worse when I was at home. Even though our first home was payed off in 1997, and this new home was way better and had such a small mortgage (and so very little financial debt), my earnings obviously took a lot of pressure off of him to perform. I recall this being an issue after our first daughter was born in 1991. I was something of a career woman, and before I had her, I didn't think going back to work full time would be that big of a deal. It was. I wanted to be with her as much as possible. I recall saying to my husband then that I wanted to find part-time work. He flipped out. Looking back, that was a very telling sign of the way he thought of himself as a provider for his family. I was very good with our finances, and earned a good bonus from work, and that is how our first home was payed off in nine years. Additionally, I enjoyed working outside the home, at least part time. Unfortunately, working part time at my main place of employment was not possible.

September 10, 2001 was my first day back at work. The department hadn't had a supervisor for over three months, so the place was in poor shape, with staff needing to be hired and so on. Thank goodness for the Reiki, because it really helped me feel relaxed and able to get what needed to be done done. I hired more staff and things gradually improved. I was able to buy stuff the children needed. Even though I had saved $10,000 for the extra time I was off, on top of the six-month maternity leave, I hadn't counted on Hope being unable to adjust well to the germs at the daycare, or how that would affect me being able to go back to work.

I knew that being unable to earn enough might very well mean that I would have to leave my home with all three kids, and I had to be prepared to do that. Time had passed, and I was feeling much stronger. The Reiki really helped me to relax with all the challenges I was facing. You see, I had family in town, but they never offered any help, even though they knew full well how hard things were on me and the kids. It was like they either were stupid and didn't know how to help, or they were making me pay for the mistake I had made of marrying the wrong person—a person I only married because of how they raised me! This family of mine was indeed something else!

I had never wallowed in the depths of self-pity, nor was I the chronic complainer type, but I would ask for help when I needed it. They raised me that way too. Due to the lack of concern from my immediate family, and with my extended family being fairly fragmented (very much out of what was normal), I often needed help. They must have seen how much I struggled, and in a weird sort of way, they seemed to enjoy it. Is that what the Jehovah Witnesses teach? I have heard that some religions like the fact that people suffer. They seem to think it brings people closer to God. I think they are closer to stupidity and self-righteousness. That is so unloving in my eyes.

I recall, long after my husband and I had split, I asked my mom why they never helped me when I needed it. She replied, "You never looked like you needed help." Some people are just so blind to what they don't want to see in themselves. There were many times, when I had no other option, I would have to ask them for help. Their reply was always that they had shopping or something else to do. Getting them to say yes to me about anything took way too much work. It was easier just to do it myself.

I think that good decent people do whatever they can to do better by their kids than their parents did by them. I know I did, and as I looked back, it's a big reason why my kids turned out so well, despite these really huge challenges. I was certainly paying attention to my kids in a real way, at least until they were all turned against me when they turned twelve or thirteen years of age. I later learned from a professional that my kids and I were the victims of what is called "parental alienation."

Family court and judges need to be aware of this manipulation, something that can be done by either parent, and sometimes through the lawyers, who see this as a means to extract more resources from families.

Someone came to me and said that my ex-husband's new lawyer was the same lawyer the Winnipeg police use when they need to be represented about some indiscretion. When does the hurting stop?? You get away from an abusive marriage single-handedly, and then the court system supports the abuser in turning your children against you, treating his own children as pawns to get back at you for wanting to leave the abusive situation. Seems like the government obviously doesn't want women to get out of abusive situations, no matter what they say or do otherwise. I understand that parental alienation does happen to Dad's as well. The point here is that emotionally healthy parents do not do this to their children, and it's up to the family law sector to spot this and nip it in the bud. Otherwise, they are taking part in the abuse, and it becomes just a confusing mess for everyone. The psychologist I saw for years after my separation just said this: "It sounds like your parenting is being undermined, and that is harmful to the children." Therapists aren't even fully trained in dealing with parental alienation. It wasn't until 2012 that I learned it even had a name.

You may wonder how I managed through all of this? That's a good question. I would say that what helped me the most was knowing that it wasn't my fault, and that I am a loveable woman—no matter what they say about me. People project their own fears and demons on you without even being conscious of it. All I say is that I'd like to se anyone else walk in my shoes with the options available, and then tell me. Our children were the number one top priority for me.

By August 2002, my department at work was in much better condition and running smoothly. I had hired some good staff at that store, and it just took some time and dedication to get things coming around. That September, Alex was headed into grade six, with the younger two still in daycare. For the first time in about a year, since I had returned to work in September of 2001, the HR Department was starting to question me about my "family situation." I had missed ten days of work that year, three of which were in July 2002, when both Hope and Andrew got the chicken pox and I was home with them three days in a row. Hope actually went to the daycare often when she should have been at home. Hope was put on a low dose antibiotic, and I think all that weakened her immune system further. Her one-on-one special-needs worker at the daycare could take her to quiet locations in the daycare, which helped.

That month, we took a week off as a family and went to a friend's cabin near Winnipeg Beach. The weather couldn't have been better, and it sure was great to out of the city. This was a first with Hope. I had taken her to beaches for the day, but this was a whole week, with us all away together as a family. I say rare because my husband didn't like being in nature or being away from home very much. We had done a good amount of these activities before we had children, so I didn't see why we couldn't continue that and show the kids the beauty of nature. That was the best part of what I could recall about my childhood, so why wouldn't I want my kids to know how much fun you can have at our province's many lakes and beaches? I mostly had to take the kids to the beach and other outings on my own.

As I mentioned before, at that time Alex was headed for grade six in September. I was so proud of how she was growing up. She was active in her keyboard lessons and had been playing indoor and outdoor soccer since she was eight. I loved going to her games to watching her play. I still wish that I could have found a way for her to stay in synchronized swimming. She did that for one year when she was about six years old, but when the club's schedule changed from swimming one hour a week to three and a half hours, the times simply interfered with my working hours. She was a beautiful swimmer, and very strong as well.

Anyway, getting back to the daycare situation, Hope would have missed many more days had I not been allowed to still take her in when she was not feeling at her best. When Hope and Andrew contracted chicken pox at the same time, I was relieved that they at least got them at the same time, or I would have missed twice as much time.

Hope has very small ear canals, and it didn't take much for them to get infected, even with the surgery that was done to open them to drain. She was on a small daily dose of antibiotics for quite a while, and I think this caused a lot of problems with her immune system. It really messed up her body's biome as well, because she suffered many yeast infections (especially around her gastrostomy site, including her entire stomach area). So, in addition to my company putting pressure on me about missing work, I had Hope, whose body was being destroyed by too many antibiotics, which weren't working to kill the infections, but were actually increasing them.

Human resources treated me as though I were some sort of huge liability to them now, with my "family situation," even after eighteen years of service and a spotless record of mutual benefit. I did good work, encouraged my peers around me to do the same, mentored many who wanted to move up in the company, and this was my reward? *As soon as I need some help, I am discarded?* I spoke with a few friends, who urged me to contact the Human Rights Department (I'm pretty sure that is a federal department in our government). I needed my career and my income there to pay for my mortgage, living expenses, daycare, food, taxes, and everything else. I was literally doing the best I could. What else could I do? What would you do in the same situation?

It was mid November 2002 when my husband finally decided to go to his first AA meeting. It had been over a year of his workmate picking him up at home and driving him to work every day, because as I've said, he had lost his driver's licence in Sept 2000. That's how long it took for him to realize he needed help. As much as his workmate was helpful in terms of the chauffeur service to and from work, it no doubt enabled him to ignore the reason why he didn't have his licence. I drove him to his first AA meeting, and for several days after that, but asked that he find another lift to and from meetings, because I needed to get the kids their dinner and help them with homework, bath time, etc. It was their life too!

It was a reasonable request, and although I fully supported him getting sober, he had to honor my request to find some other way to get there. He did have a bike in the garage after all. In other words: Take responsibility! That's what I have been doing all along. I checked with my sponsor in Al-Anon and she agreed. The people in AA love to help newcomers find sobriety. It's the glue that keeps them sober, because it reminds them how far they have come. My job was keeping the children in the best shape possible, because their needs needed to come first for them to grow up into happy, responsible, reliable people.

Sometime around the middle of November, 2002, I came home after picking up the kids from daycare and had started getting dinner ready when I remembered there was laundry in the washing machine. I went downstairs to transfer it into the dryer when my husband came downstairs and asked me to drive him to his meeting. I said I couldn't. The next thing I knew, the door was shut and he was in the laundry room with me, *demanding* that I drive him. I still don't know how I managed to get out of there without being hit. His eyes looked blank, like he wasn't even there. I just stared into his eyes as I slowly inched my way towards the door. By this time, Andrew was looking for me, and I could hear him coming down the stairs. I opened the door, grabbed Andrew (who was just outside the door), ran up the stairs, and called his parents.

I told them I was calling them instead of the police. They came right away to take their son to his meeting. Our children hadn't seen much conflict of any kind during our marriage. But don't think that they didn't intuitively know that things weren't quite right. The last year together as a family, our eldest daughter and I were both sick with the flu at the same time. We were both in bed with buckets on either side of us. It was at this time that I broke the news to her that her parents were going to separate.

Alex, who was in grade six at the time, said, "Well, that should have happened a long time ago." Out of the mouths of babes. I was stunned. Don't think that, just because you're not fighting, your kids are not feeling the tension in your relationship, because you can bet they are, especially if they are girls.

All of our immune systems were way down during this time, and as I look back at this now, I'm sure it was due to the negative energy in the home. She and I were both concerned about where it was all going. I had to make the change. Nothing would change for the better unless I did.

It was the very next day that I asked my husband to leave, and I gave him a week. He was gone in three days. When he left that morning, November 22, 2002, he said that he was sorry, and I was able to say that I forgave him. He wasn't a bad guy, but over the years, he failed to deal with things in a healthy way, and this was where that takes you. Places you never thought you would be. I had to put the children's safety as top priority. It was sad to see what our marriage had turned into, but you either grow together through challenges or you move apart. It wasn't my first choice, but it was the reason I got the help I needed to do my part and to let go of the parts I had no control over. That is the key to sanity. Letting go of what you cannot control.

There had been countless times we had talked about this issue as a couple, but nothing was ever done with any sort of consistency. The only way this much needed change was going to happen was if I *made* the change happen, and that's what it all came down to. Tony was never going to make the change on his own. The years of drinking destroyed the love that I once had, and truthfully, after Hope's birth, I no longer thought I was the one who would help him see that there was a reason to change. I was certain of that, and let that go too.

Women think they can change a man, but you can't. They have to see a reason to change, and you can save yourself a lot of strife by knowing that truth. I was determined that the years of broken promises were not going to become broken bones, and that was where I feared it was headed. That said, he was always very careful not to let the children hear him say nasty things to me—things designed to keep me in fear of standing in my truth. I think he avoided it because he had told me many times (long before we had kids of our own) how much it had hurt him when he heard his own parents fight. It was a no brainer for me, because I didn't like the feeling when my parents fought either. However, we cannot be blind to the fact that children can easily pick up the vibes of a relationship that is struggling, even though they aren't seeing or hearing any yelling.

While I didn't want to see my husband become destitute, I did want to get my share of the marriage contents and make a new life without him. When I had started back at Al-Anon a year earlier, I had wanted to separate. I could recall all the times he had promised to get help with his drinking and didn't. It had sure seemed like something that wasn't possible on his own, because he had tried so many times to quit and it just hadn't stuck. Obviously, he needed to follow a program to unravel all those character defects that allowed alcohol to just take over his whole life, affecting those around him. Actually going to meetings and admitting to others that he had a problem meant that it wasn't too late for him, but I knew that it was too late for us

I didn't let this come between my children and their other grandparents, because that is what children need and deserve: grandparents who cared. As I believe I have mentioned, my parents joined the Jehovah Witnesses in 1990, for some reason, right about the time when we got married. They rarely purchased birthday gifts or Christmas presents for the kids. They never offered to babysit, and when they occasionally agreed to, they always complained about something, like my being late coming home. They just made it so you didn't want to ask them. It literally was from one extreme to another. His parents were happy to stay with them to the wee hours of the morning.

CHAPTER 10

More Healing

Shortly after my husband and I split up in the third week of November 2002, it was easy to feel the energy shift. I felt like I could leap tall buildings with a single bound. Seriously, I felt like my own superhero! Hope was five at the time, not yet walking, but seemed to get sick a lot less often, even during those winter months, which had always been the worst on her. There was lots of laughter. Alex started having friends over again, and the house was filled with activity! One week after my husband agreed to leave, the HR department at my work had another interview with me. This time, feeling more self-assured, I asked for a settlement. Being that I had already made contact with the Human Rights Department (HRD) about their issue with my missing ten days of work that year, while raising Hope with all her challenges (which is completely acceptable at some workplaces), I found the courage to ask. I sure wish the HRD had given me better advice though, because my employer seemed pretty quick to write a $20,000 cheque. HRD told me I could ask for $1000 for every year worked. I sure found out how bad that advice was!

My employer lost a huge asset to their company. I had started there in 1985 and been quickly fast-tracked into management. I was offered the assistant district manager position in January 1989, just four months after purchasing my first home in Winnipeg. I turned it down. The company had just moved their head office to Calgary, buying up the head-office employees' homes so that they would have the capitol to buy new homes in Vancouver. I wasn't a head-office employee, and they weren't interested in purchasing my home so I could make the move to Vancouver. Sure, I could have taken that position and sold my home, but I would have lost my down payment in the process, and the real-estate market was very stagnant during that time. Besides, if I would have gone, I wouldn't have had my kids. I had yet to get married at that time, and he would not have moved with me. I knew that. Hindsight is 20/20. Of course, it always is.

I knew I had to get Hope's health back to normal, and that meant she could no longer take any antibiotics. If she did get sick, I would have to keep her home. Her diet was already quite good. She never ate any sugary foods, so as soon as the antibiotics were stopped, her health improved dramatically. By the end of that year, she didn't get sick any more or less than her peers. Looking back at this, it seems clear that it was the antibiotics that destroyed her immune system.

In early 2003, being off healing allowed me some well-deserved time and attention for myself. I continued the healing with Reiki and started to learn more about meditation, yoga, and Pilates. I swam three time a week and started to get in very good shape, fitness-wise. Alex continued to play soccer year-round and take keyboard lessons, and I had both Hope and Andrew in swimming lessons. Having this extra time for myself to heal really helped. During this year off, I started to look at what I was going to do for income. Working in schools with special-needs children seemed like a good fit for me and my family. As well, having this personal experience, I felt made me more in tune with these special kids. I certainly had hundreds of one-on-one hours with the therapists from SMD who saw Hope before school during those first five years of her life. That taught me a lot about children with special needs, and the common threads that exist between all disabilities.

I applied with the school division and was told that the way one starts is as a substitute, when someone calls in sick. I wasn't getting very many calls, just one or maybe two a week. The most I ever worked was three days a week. So, while I waited to be called to work in the schools, I subbed at the children's daycare when they needed help. Finding another part-time job, one that was flexible enough to work with the iffy situation with the school, was very challenging. It would have been the best situation for me and my children's schedule.

I did that as long as I could. Trying to piece together an income here and there, with nothing stable, was nerve wracking. I ended up finding a part-time, outside sales position. Selling the product—pre-arranged funerals—was definitely not my idea of fulfilling work. The hours were flexible though, because I could set up my own appointments. From what I observed of the other salespeople there, three months was the average tenure. I stayed for a year.

In January 2005, the kids were at school and the daycare, and I was at home sitting in my kitchen. I heard someone open the front door and walk into the house, moving straight into the bathroom. I was shocked to see that it was my ex-husband. It was not hard to tell that he had been drinking. He started yelling at me, asking why our separation was taking so long and blaming me for stalling on it. I had already fired one lawyer for taking her time, and it appeared the situation was continuing with my new one. He said that he was going to the daycare to get the kids. I called there right away to warn the staff and got into my car to follow him. When I got thier I could see his girlfriends car parked on the wrong side of the road. He walked into the daycare intoxicated and tried to take our children out of there. He fled the scene and I called the police who told me to go to the Law Courts and get a protection order. They gave me a paper called Charateristics of an Abuser. posted a copy here.

CHARACTERISTICS OF AN ABUSER

_____ Probably witnessed abuse or was abused as a child.

_____ Possessive and jealous--often imagines you are having affairs. May be jealous of family, friends or even own children.

_____ Bad temper--either flares up over every little thing or lets anger build and then explodes.

_____ Blames others. Does not accept responsibility for his/her anger or actions.

_____ Tells you it's all your fault: projects own faults onto you (If you didn't do this I wouldn't...)

_____ May blame alcohol and/or drugs for abusive behaviour (Well, I was drinking...I didn't know what I was doing).

_____ Jeckyl and Hyde personalities. Charming to people outside the family and tries to keep abuse hidden.

_____ Has rigid ideas of the roles of men and women (A man is the head of the house, the woman is expected to do what he tells her to).

_____ May have other problems with the law.

_____ May behave in a threatening or intimidating way (ie. weapons, punches holes in walls, etc.)

_____ Tries to isolate you. discourages you from seeing friends and family. May discourage you from working or getting better education.

_____ Tries to control your behaviour, and may try to control your thoughts through _brainwashing_ techniques.

_____ Verbal abuse (insults, put-downs, name calling).

_____ Whatever you do, he/she says it's wrong.

_____ Will do whatever it takes to drive you away and whatever it takes to get you back--grab the kids or apologize profusely, send flowers, take you out for dinner, very real tears, promise anything (knows exactly what you want to hear: I'll go to church, I'll go to counselling, I'll stop drinking, I'll never hit you again, etc.)

_____ Promises to change, but never does.

_____ When physical abuse occurs it often follows a pattern.

_____ Minimizes the seriousness of the abuse or may deny it completely.

_____ After an explosion, he/she feels better and can't understand why you remain angry or upset.

Seriously? This is just an absurd system. Nothing seems to link up together in a way that's good for children. I don't know who or what is more insane, the lawyers or the system! _What?_ Seems like everyone is just enabling the insanity to continue! It was beginning to look like the system was abusive. Or was it the people in the system? What does it look like to you? It certainly is ass backwards. It's no wonder our social systems have become so over-burdened. The system is designed to *put* someone in a crisis.

Our children continue to be picked up every second weekend by my ex's girlfriend. When Alex came back one weekend, she said this to me: "Dad thinks it would be a good idea for me to live two weeks with him and two weeks with you."

Since he had just moved to the city with his girlfriend, from the country where they had been living for the past few years, this could have worked, but they lived in the north end of the city and we were living in the south end. Alex's school, friends, and activities were all in the south end. I told Alex that everything she needed was here for her, and besides, her father shouldn't be speaking through her about what he thought was a good idea. Family Court insists that parents take a program called "For the Sake of the Children" and they tell parents never to do that. We could speak with *each other* about the kids. I spoke with my lawyer about this, and she said, "Tell her to pick. She's not going to choose him." Well she did!

Last time I listen to a lawyer. Alex was thirteen at the time, and she and I have never spent any significant time together since. I continued to only work part-time sales-rep jobs, or whatever else I could find, so that I could be as close to her school as possible, as often as possible, so I could pick her up and talk with her. She quit all her activities when she moved to her father's.

Everyone said that she wouldn't stay. In fact, I had one friend whose daughter had done the same thing, and she had returned after only two months. Alex was promised a cell phone if she moved. This was 2005, and not many people had cell phones. My family budget allowed for her year-round soccer and music lessons, but adding a cell phone was something I wasn't going to do. Heck, even I didn't have one at that time.

Alex moved there sometime in July 2005. I have no recollection of that day she took all her clothes, etc. We all missed Alex so much. When Andrew started kindergarten that September, the class all made family portraits. I was shocked at a parent/teacher event when I saw that the picture Andrew made just had me and him in it. It was after that meeting that I asked the guidance councillor if Andrew could join in on the Gem's group his sister Alex had participated in. This was small group of students, from families healing after separation/divorce, who met once a cycle. She replied that it wasn't in the budget. I had never heard of anything so ridiculous. She was still employed full time at that school!

Continuing with the Reiki trainings, I received my third and master level in the summer of 2005. My instructor told me that lots of her students go on and set up their own practices in their homes. I thought this would be great and suit the children's schedule well. If Hope were too sick to go to daycare or school, it would be perfect, as I would already be at home. Incidentally, I completed hypnosis trainings in 2011, and now had a master's level in both. Starting a home-based business using these modalities didn't happen easily.

I also studied Huna Kane, a Hawaiian massage that basically uses words, working on the premise that our beliefs, and therefore emotions, lodge themselves in specific areas in our bodies. The practitioner massages the client while saying specific phrases for specific areas in order to help facilitate the release of repressed emotion. While neither of these trainings turned into any sort of income generation at that time, my full-time career transition continued.

In August 2006, I got a full-time management position at Starbucks. It was at this same time that our separation agreement finally went through. The whole legal-marriage breakup seemed to take longer than other people's I knew. After a few months, Starbucks started scheduling me on the weekends when I had my children, after they had agreed to me working only every second weekend. That switched to no weekends off. I was just a short time with Starbucks, and then started part time as a sales representative, twenty-four hours each week, plus mileage. This allowed me to go back on the sub list at school, as that was my preference of employment. I could get one day each week at school, while fitting in the price audits any time during the week. That was the beauty of that job. During that time, I still applied for several posted positions at the school, but it was all done by seniority. Without it, others with more tenure got the positions.

CHAPTER 11

Volunteering and Advocating

Since my departure from full-time work in Nov. 2002, I had been volunteering, first with the Society of Manitobans with Disabilities, mostly selling their Great Escape Lottery tickets, and then later with The Children's Wish, wrapping Christmas presents at Winners. I also volunteered at Variety Club and did various things at the school and daycare. I made it known to the various agencies that I was also looking for work that would fit my schedule with my children. I attended and got involved with other special-needs groups, hoping that through that networking a full-time position that fit my family would soon turn up. Nothing ever did. I also let the government know how ass backwards their system was. Foster families were being financially compensated to help manage their children's special needs, yet biological families had to fight for everything. Makes no sense. It's ridiculous!

In the community where I lived, I met a couple with a blended family who were fostering two boys with cerebral palsy, each from a different agency, and were receiving $8000 each month to care for the boys. The most help I ever got was after Andrew was born, when I asked for and received twenty-four respite hours a week until September 2000. After that, respite hours were reduced to fourteen hours a week. The family that fostered was shocked when she learned how little I got as the biological parent, even though the child's needs do not change. It's criminal basically.

Then I started to take part in Community Livings Mb retreats, advocating for services for special-needs families at home and in school. I recall one time, while waiting for a clinic at the Rehab Centre for Children on Wellington Cres, there was a man in the waiting room with a small child the same age as Hope. The child couldn't sit up and was rolling on the floor. I could see that he had a gastrostomy tube like Hope has. We got to talking, and he told me that his family fosters special-needs kids, and that it was their way to buy lots of special things for their family.

That experience always stayed with me. The contrast. Here was me doing whatever I could do to make my daughter's life as good as possible. She wasn't the child rolling around everyone's snow boots; she was sitting on my lap with a story being read to her. And here was this guy letting the child roll on the dirty floor while he bragged to me about the snowmobiles, jet ski's, and other stuff his family gets to buy because of the big dollars he earns. Brutal system we have here. Most tax payers would be shocked at the abuses in the system. It amounts to human trafficking. At the other end of social ills, along my travels, I found this site and wanted to share it: www.itnj.org. Check it out.

CHAPTER 12

The Set Back

As none of these volunteering endeavours turned into a paid position, I continued working at various part-time (mostly sales rep) positions, while still applying for positions at the school. It was at this same time (approximately March 2007) when Hope was put on a medication by her neurologist. This medication affected her sleep so she woke up every three hours every night, stopped swallowing and walking, and started to frequently pull out her feeding tube. It all started when Hope was in grade three. Every time she was in the gym (sitting on the bench with her special-needs assistant) with the other children, who were running around the gym to warm up, the faculty started to notice that Hope would stretch out her arms and legs, then release that stretch and laugh. Concerned, the school would write about this in her communication book.

I would respond by telling them about when I met with about twenty-five other families in Minneapolis. A parent there had mentioned that her daughter had started to walk on her own after doing lots of those same stretching exercises. Since Hope was almost due for her yearly check up with the neurologist, I thanked the school for their concern, but told them I was sure it was nothing to be concerned about. I told them I felt that Hope was simply responding to the joy and laughter in the room, that created some energy Hope was picking up on, joining in the only way she knew how. It didn't mean a medication change was needed, but that is what happened with catastrophic results.

Exhibit C

Kim James
615 Manchester Blvd. N
Winnipeg, Mb.
R3T 1N9

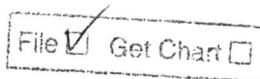

File ☑ Get Chart ☐

January 21, 2008

Re: Hope James's medication change in early 2007.

Although some verbal conversations have taken place I now am writing a letter, and finally have the strength to do so to those concerned outlining the sequence of events that were involved with changing Hope's medication, and to document how Hope and her family have been affected by NOT being listened to in the first place. It involves Hope stretching out her arms and legs for a few seconds several times each day. This is a behavior I have seen Hope do many times and have not been concerned with it being seizure activity. While respecting your professionalism, it does has an impact.

In the summer of 2004 while in Minneapolis visiting with other families I talked with another Mom whose child did the same exercise and it preceded that child walking. This proved to be true with Hope as well. By 2006 Hope was walking on her own for short distances and much longer if she could hold hands. In late 2006 and early 2007, the school became very focussed on this stretching out as being seizures and I was getting the message that they thought I was not taking it very seriously. The school called the neurologist Dr. ████ without my knowledge and when I took Hope to the appt with Dr ████. Many people from the school were already there waiting for Hope and I to arrive. I felt very "ganged up" upon at this appointment.

In point form this is how the medication change affected Hope:
- waking every 2 hours each and every night.
-stopped oral feeding completely
-pulling out her feeding tube, thus it closing up
-stopped walking
-suddenly burst into tears

Hope waking up several times each night had the obvious and detrimental effect on her family. The lack of sleep consistently over the better part of a year exhausted me, thus affecting everyone else. Raising a child with this level of need is hard enough as it is without this extra aggrivation. A bed enclosure was ordered in attempt to at least contain her in bed when she woke. It has taken me literally months to re-gain my sleep schedule due to this, not to mention the extra energy to write this letter. Hope did end up having a seizure in Nov.2007. I called Dr ████ who was not available. I called Dr ████ and asked to give instructions to wean off the lamotragene and put her back on the clobazam. Hope is gradually getting back to where she was with sleeping walking eating etc. Parents of children with disabilities are often told they know their children best. Please remember this next time.

Sincerely,

Kim James

.cc Dr. ████
.cc Dr. ████
.cc ████
.cc Mr. ████
.cc ████ Student Services Co-ordinator ████

After several months of Hope being on this new medication, I learned that it was prescribed for bipolar disorder. Hope is not bipolar, which is why the medication didn't work for her. She didn't need the medication in the first place. The new meds she was taking never stopped a seizure. Hope only got seizures when she had a fever. Please note: Never start taking medications until you've googled all you can about it, or asked your pharmacist. Never take the doctor's word as gospel. There was no need to change her medication anyways, because her stretching out her arms and legs had nothing to do with seizures and everything to do with her muscles really waking up, feeling stronger and wanting to move. This medication change, which lasted several months, set her back as least a year, in terms of trying to regain the milestones lost during that time.

That was January 2008. I wrote the above letter to explain the situation to the professionals who help direct the care for Hope on a daily basic, and help them understand how this sort of issue can impact a family. By March 2008, I was laid off from my part-time price-audit sales position, which really had been the best job I had found in terms of working with my family's schedule, because it was so flexible. I started applying for three jobs every day, hoping something would pan out.

Bills were piling up, as I really concentrated on my mortgage payment, prop, taxes, daycare for Hope, and food. In May 2008, the Liquor Mart hired me as a cashier. I was grateful to get this position, which offered not quite full-time hours. I told them I could only work every other weekend because I had my kids with me. They agreed. Once again, just like at Starbucks, I was scheduled opposite to what we had agreed on when they were hiring me. As a result, I didn't make it through the probation period. This brought me back to square one, looking for work. I must have applied for a hundred and fifty jobs by March, which was totalling nerve wracking.

I ended up having to put my home on the market to sell. I was behind in my payments to Revenue Canada, paying back the child tax credit which I had continued collecting for my oldest daughter Alex after she moved to her father's house in 2005. Prior to deciding to sell, I applied for more jobs. It was so sad putting my house on the market, not knowing where I was going to live, not sleeping well from all the stress, and not sure where Hope was going. Due to her mobility needs, after she stopped walking, it wasn't easy finding something that would accommodate her. Talk about a stressful situation! This had to be the worst. I even started smoking cigarettes after being smoke free for decades. I recognised the problem, and even though I knew I was responding to this huge stress with cigarettes, I got a hypnosis appointment to deal with it, and I haven't had a cigarette since.

I was having discussions with Children Special Services (who provided respite, other requirements for school, daycare, etc.). I informed Hope's worker that I would have to sell my home, and I was not sure if any new place I could get would accommodate Hope, as she wasn't walking at the time. Hope had always lived in a single dwelling home with me, so we never had to deal with flights of stairs, etc. Since I wasn't a candidate to purchase another home right then, due to being unemployed, I was looking for an apartment with a one-year lease, reasonably close to Andrew's school. Hope's case worker asked Hope's father if he would consider taking Hope during this time. This is eventually what did happen, and looking back on this now, I find it interesting that he had to be asked. That's a good indicator of why our marriage failed: I was in it alone. My ex's relationship with his girlfriend was ending at that time, and so he moved into his parents' home and took Hope with him. Andrew and I rented a two-bedroom apartment on Pembina Hwy, July 1, 2008. That day, we had a yard sale, after the movers had moved our stuff. We had left a four-bedroom bungalow, and there was only so much that would fit into a small two-bedroom apartment. It meant leaving a lot of our life behind.

CHAPTER 13

More losses

While Andrew and I moved into the apartment July 2008, I didn't start working until September 2008. I picked up another sales-rep part-time job as a merchandiser, with a flexible option, which was good. Having the summer off before work started was also good, and I got to spend time at the beach recovering from all the stress. I found this time of my life to be very traumatic. It all started in 2005 when Alex moved, and now Hope was gone too. Hope not living with me at this time had nothing to do with my wishes, desires, or capabilities. It had to do solely with the dwelling that I had to live in at that time. I recall going through an emotional upheaval, because now, for the first time, looking back at the situation with "fresh eyes", I couldn't help wondering why something wasn't offered to me at that time to help Hope stay with me. What the hell were those first ten and a half years of raising her all about? Where was the sense in making me, her mother, struggle to provide care for her with barely any support, receiving nothing near what a foster parent would get to do the same job?

Let's just say that's the way the system is: reactionary, dealing only with crisis situations. Nothing preventative seems to be done, or focused on eliminating government dependency. There are so many agencies, all fragmented and ineffective, and I often found myself without any real support on any level. Real support to me would look like promoting a work/life balance that would accommodate the extraordinary needs of parenting a child with difficulties. Depending on the condition or disability, it could also look like providing needed full-time attention, and if that were the case, why support a foster parent in doing just that after denying the very capable biological parent first?

Hope would have gone into foster care in June 2008, if her father hadn't agreed to take her. He went to live with his parents, so he would have help from his family while outside respite was being figured out. While living in the apartment, I would take Hope on special occasions like Christmas, Easter, etc. I did visit her at least once a week too, as Hope was finishing her last year at her elementary school. Hope had a fabulous educational experience at that school for the most part. The neighbourhood, the school ... everyone knew Hope. I had worked my whole life to get into a neighborhood as great as that one—the one we had to leave. Not having Hope with me was hard after those ten and a half years of really giving it all ... and then losing it all. I took a baby home from the hospital and I loved her, and I thought I would be able to give her the very best of what she needs. I felt totally ripped off! Beyond words. Ripped off. I felt so used by a system that ended up offering so little help while making it impossible to meet the needs and rights of a child.

The sad fact here is that I was then forced to sign Hope over to her father, who didn't really want to take her or he would have offered, so that the government could fulfil their goal of being 100 percent ineffective in dealing with the social issues of this situation. What could have been different and prevented this situation, which really is a crisis situation? People should not have to choose money over their own children. Why is it the government only sees the financial component to raising a child in a fostering situation, and this same support is not offered to a biological parent? Why did I go through so many darn services workers when other parents that I knew of always had the same one? I stopped counting at ten. What worker could ever get in touch with and really know their clients when they were changing clients all the time? People need time to get to know each other. You don't want to be in our social system if you want to enjoy a peaceful serene life. It sadly leads to resignation, saying, "I'll do it myself," because just asking seems to be way too much of a waste of time, remembering the other times you asked and the outcomes. What people don't know is that they *don't know*.

August 28, 2016

Dear Go Public

The stories I've read since recently discovering this CBC are as shocking as the one I will inform you of. In October 1997, I gave birth to my second child. At her birth is was discovered that she was a rare genetic syndrome which was diagnosed at 3 weeks called Wolf Hirschhorn Syndrome or 4P- Syndrome. This non-hereditary syndrome is characterized by low birth weight (in her case 3.5 lbs) seizures, feeding difficulties and very slow development sometimes heart and renal problems. Hope did not have the heart and renal issues, however had a bilateral cleft palate which greatly affected her feeding plus had numerous grand mal seizures between the ages of 9 months to around 3 years. I tried to learn everything I could because the Drs here in Winnipeg Mb had never seen this before. This baby named Hope stayed at St Boniface Hospital where she was delivered October 30th for 5 weeks coming home Dec.7th at 5lbs. I was told there was lots of help in the community. The social worker in the hospital at that time also said you wouldn't be a bad person if I left her there. I am an attentive Mom and leaving a child that I loved for 9 months gestation didn't seem like something I wanted to do. Besides her then almost 6 years old sister was lovingly singing songs to my growing belly for 9 months, so telling her that her baby sister wasn't good enough to bring home so leaving her at the hospital was not an option.

Life had changed enormously. This is a parent's worst nightmare. Most people do not have a clue what they have and don't even get me started on how people could abuse children. Today, Hope is coming up for 19. When I went back to work in July 1998, she was cared for by her Grandparents because the special need daycare was over 1200.00 per month and across the city from where I worked. Her physical health was quite good and I would make her therapy appts on my day off mid week. Life was exhausting, yet became routine. She spent several days in intensive care after her half dozen grand mal seizures that went status. This means they gave her so many drugs to stop the seizure, it also stopped respiration. Hope was also placed with a gastronomy tube for feeding in Nov.2000.

Respite was offered at started at 4 hours per week. I constantly asked for more help and eventually attained a total of 20 hours per week that was cut back to 14 hours. In 2002 after being in a public daycare for a year because her Grandparents were entering their 80's, I had to stop working full time because the top of the line anti-biotic wasn't working and she was constantly catching infections. On the advice of friends and co-workers I called the Human Rights Commission to tell my story. Everyone who knew me was shocked at what little help was offered despite my constant pleas for help. The HRC advised me that I could ask for a buyout and asking 1000.00 for each year of work was advised. All I knew is that this couldn't continue. I was being harassed for a circumstance I was deceived into accepting. I asked for 20, 000.00 after 20 years of management with a large retail chain. They wrote a cheque on the spot.

I took the next year off to get her healthy and I am happy to say she stayed healthy even in daycare. Finding full time work again proved not so easy so I worked part time. In 2008, I was laid off from my time sales rep position and was forced to sell the home I had worked the majority of my life for.

You might ask where all the help was in the community was that I was told in Dec 1997? I'm telling you it didn't exist. When I was laid off from the part time position (min wage pay) as a part time sales rep with no benefits pension etc., I called the social worker at St. Boniface Hospital. I told her she needs to tell parents to inform the hospital admin staff that they are NOT going to take a baby home with high medical/special needs until they have the same support a foster parent/s would get. My friends urged me to go public with CBC about this in 2000. I wrote letters to the NDP government (gov at the time)with no action.

Years later when Hope was about 6 or 7, I learned from neighbour who fostered 2 boys with cerebral palsy. These boys like Hope were tube fed , diapered, history of seizures and non ambulatory earned 4000.00 a month tax free. Can you imagine how betrayed I felt when they showed me those cheques?

Sincerely,

Kim Parke

CHAPTER 14

Rebuilding ... again!

When Andrew and I moved into the apartment, it was a first for him, and for me as well really. I had never lived in an apartment with children before. They were used to playing outside in the back yard, and I was used to being able to keep an eye on them even though I might have been in the house for a moment. Luckily, winter came and that wasn't so much of an issue anymore, but it was a long, cold winter. I worked as a merchandiser, travelling from store to store and setting up and filling displays. Early the next year, at the end of February, I took Alex and Andrew to Playa del Carmen in Mexico for one week. We had a great week off together. It was Alex's graduating year from high school.

The spring of 2009 was interesting, because it felt like a new beginning. The apartment that we moved into had an outdoor pool, which had been closed when we moved because of repairs. These repairs were done now and Andrew and I got a few swims in before we moved into our new house, which I purchased in the neighbourhood. I spotted this house for sale on my way to view another property, which was in another area and not really suitable in other ways. This one on Jubilee was a good stable home, in the area I had wanted, but a lot smaller than I would have preferred. With only two weeks left in June, I didn't have all the time in the world to look for a home because my lease was almost up.

I had owned a home since I was twenty-four, and prolonged apartment living wasn't something I was planning on doing at this stage of my life. The house on Jubilee wasn't the best house I looked at in the spring of 2009, it was simply the best one that I could get in the time frame I was dealing with. Even if Alex wanted to ever move back in with me, which she was always 100 percent welcome to do, she couldn't have, because I couldn't find a home for sale big enough in my price range that was available. If I'd had the income from whatever source, such as government assistance with raising a child with special needs, I would never have had to sell my home in the first place. It's that simple. That was the house I had worked for since my early twenties, specifically to get myself into a neighbourhood like that.

When I took Hope home from the hospital in December of 1997, I believed them when they said, "There is a lot of help out there in the community." People who work in these positions are so out of touch with reality. You may be able to access some resources from various non-profits who legitimately care for special-needs children, but there is no help for the nuts and bolts of day to day living, unless you've been able to sue your doctor and reach a settlement that will set you up financially for the challenges of raising someone with complex needs.

letter to Hospital   1/3

I am here before you to share my experiences following the birth of my second daughter named Hope on October 30,1997.

I will describe as briefly as possible what happened after I arrived at the hospital the early morning of Oct. 30, 1997, what I experienced in the hours after the birth that same day and what I recommend to the patient relations dept in terms of after care for high medical needs births at this hospital.

On Oct. 30, 1997, Hope was born via c-section @ 6:42 am. C-section was recommended due to the baby's heart de-celerating during contractions. Baby was brought to my side for a moment minutes after delivery, then taken to intensive care for observation and diagnosis. I was taken to a recovery post partum area where there was a large family also present surrounding another newborn, I was left alone, there with little to no care until I was taken to my room on the maternity ward. I have no way to convey to you just how comforting it would have been to have a medical professional spend some time speaking to me at my bedside or even providing me the comforts of a warm blankets, as I was literally shaking with shock and trauma.

This is what I experienced:

- Total shock and bewilderment of the visual presentation of baby at birth..
- In recovery nurses were absent most of the time there.
- Concern for baby.
- South American Dr. on duty came to speak to me briefly in recovery about the baby having a cleft palate and also the possibility of a syndrome but he wasn't sure. Due to the language barrier, this compounded the trauma.

This event culminates what I can only describe as the "single most horrible thing that can happen to a person.

How the trauma of Hope's birth affected me at the time. It took away my choice............thankfully only temporarily. With all the complexities of raising a child with difficulties, the untreated initial trauma immobilizes a person to barely get beyond daily tasks, numerous appts. and therapies, to even think about

letter to hospital 2/3

real" help that will propel their life in a forward progressive direction where choice is returned. I found that until I began healing with time line and hypnotherapy, I wasn't in total command of my life and the direction it was going. Once again remember the common denominator here is choice. At times in those first few months after Hope's birth, I felt as though I was living second to second. In the weeks and months that followed, amid the appts. endless series of tasks, surgeries, emergency room/resuscitation situations, intensive care stay's, I could go on and on about the repeated trauma's after the initial one. It wasn't until about the age of 3 when her health finally began to improve. Then came numerous therapies and advocating for special needs while working part time, having returned to full time work in July 1998, 9 months after Hope's birth to Mar.2. 2000. It was during my service participating as an advocate for children with disabilities that I learned that many parents there were fostering, not raising their own biological children.

After Hope's birth I was told that there was ample support and help for parent's raising children with disabilities. I didn't find that this was the case. Much of the help offered kept me in the problem rather than rising above it. I seemed to manage my life somewhat until the "real" help came when I attained knowledge of hypnosis and time line therapy in 2005. After my own healing I started to train in 2007, completed in 2011. During that 4 year period I read and practised all I could and started to create inwardaction.com my business offering hypnosis and time line to those to make real lasting change in their lives for the better, and break the patterns that no longer serve them.

I recommend that this hospital offer to all families with children born with special needs holistic complimentary and natural healing modalities and therapies 100% covered by Mb Health.

Had I received hypnosis and time line therapy in 1997, rather than 2005, I sincerely feel my life both personally, emotionally, professionally and financially would have been completely different.

I am here before you today as a woman who survived and will thrive from this event.

I appreciate the opportunity to express this to you and thank you for your time.

Yours truly,

Kim Parke

I continued to work part time until February 2010, when I was laid off from my position as a sales representative. After that, I managed to create a (somewhat) full-time sales and marketing position with a small start-up hemp company. I had found them at a local farmers market in the summer of 2009, and had contacted them to see if they were looking for help in promoting their product outside of the farmer's market. The timing was right, because even though they were ready for distribution, they didn't have marketing in place yet and I could utilize the relation-ships I had built in the grocery market industry to get their hemp line out into those venues. It was a great experience in so many ways, and I was employed there until June 2011, when that company folded and I was laid off. This was a difficult time, because I had found something that I enjoyed and was aligned with my passion for healthy people/healthy planet. I have been passionate about health and nutrition since my teens, and this was a growing industry. I thought this would have been the perfect opportunity to get into a larger home, so that Hope could come back to live with me, and Alex too if she wanted to do so. It was a hard pill to swallow.

I did a lot of soul-searching after that crushing experience and began to wonder what I should do next. I had gained so much emotional help from Reiki, hypnosis, and time-line therapy in dealing with all the stress of not only caring for a sick child but also divorce and career loss. All the things that I found helped me cope with the stress I was under, and came from me searching and taking consistent action, which helped me process all this stuff. Life can get real messy real fast when you don't deal with things as they come. Not only do you have to deal with your own messes, being in the vulnerable position of raising a child like Hope, but you also get to deal with the inadequate system, so that is placed in your lap as well.

I'll tell you, point blank, that money is the only thing I was lacking to effectively raise my daughter Hope. Those working in the system are not bad people. Some might actually be in touch with how the system is, others may know where the holes are, and still others might even see how the system itself perpetuates injustices, creating an even worse situation for families. But they all still take part as a cog in that broken system.

In July 2012, I started a business called InwardAction. Just as the name implies, its focus was healing traumas through time-line and hypnosis. I gave it a good two years, while also becoming a representative for another hemp company. I also did nutritional product demonstrations for various health-related products in nutrition stores. I eventually stopped putting my energy into my business, due to lack of customers, and went looking for a job. I was amazed at how difficult it was to get something that was full time, especially with all the work experience I had. More than a few times, I had to settle for part-time, "run of the mill" jobs that were super below my qualifications and often temporary, while still looking for something better.

I haven't mentioned my parents much at all in this book, because they really didn't see that they had any role to play in all of this. I could probably think of a million ways they could have helped my daughter at critical moments in her life that would have prevented things from getting so dire. Their minds didn't work that way. They are not solution-based people. If the government did help, it was only at a bare minimum and had nothing to do with what I really needed, which was money—money that they saw as totally legit if given to anyone outside of the child's family who could fill out an application to foster. Talk about adding insult to injury.

CHAPTER 15

What is Real Help?

Now that you have an idea of what is involved in being a biological parent of a baby born with a birth defect, you can start to have these conversations with the "powers that be" long before you or anyone you know takes that child home with them. You cannot raise a child that does not have the same medical stability as a normal child without additional support, should you find yourself unable to work outside the home. It's that simple. I found strength in my pain and chose to lead with my heart. When it comes to your children, not leading with your heart doesn't say much about the type of parent you are. Wouldn't you agree? The system we all have here is ass backwards, and yes, that is a technical term. I certainly rarely find any loving parents disagreeing with me on this. You just better be damn grateful/hopeful that nothing like this ever happens to your children.

The words you need to use are as follows: "I love this baby and can provide a healthy home setting for him/her and will see that their development is a top priority. Because of the 'unknowns' surrounding the child's life as they grow, I will require that same financial support a foster parent would receive."

I say this because you will come across the usual stuff that always happens with raising children, but if the child has complex medical needs as well, how understanding do you think your employer is going to be? Even with money being no issue, there will still be emotional upheaval. Are you ready for that? Mind you, money could certainly prevent much unnecessary emotional upheaval, by being able to maintain a comfortable home, provide good healthy food for your child to eat, and having plenty of cash to enjoy leisure and vacation time.

Personally, I would never have been able to manage as much as I did if I had not purchased a home at twenty-four, and had it payed off by 1997, ironically the same year Hope was born. Because of that clear title, our second home had a very small mortgage, with no other debt. I had been saving the maximum amount of RRSPs since my early twenties, and now all that was withdrawn in order to keep a stable home for my children from 2002 to 2008. While withdrawing on your RRSPs is not recommended, or even something I had planned to do, it was something I had to do, because I worked only part time during those years. I had saved that money to prepare for my retirement at fifty-five, rather than continuing to work for the rest of my life, which is exactly how things seem to be turning out.

Taking responsibility should not be at the expense of the person who is taking responsibility. The system is completely backwards, and I would warn anyone to not even think about doing such a thing until you have all the supports, resources, etc. that a foster family would get. The system would pay a foster family $4000 (tax free) a month for my daughter's level of need. These families wouldn't be fostering without the money, and I can honestly say I don't blame them, because doing so affects their ability to earn money outside of the home due to the needs of caring for that child, taking them to therapies, appointments, and so on. They truly need that money; however, the way the system pays out doesn't allow for "good development" in a way that is beneficial for a foster family. For example, they get less money if the child ends up walking. So, what many (or at least some) foster families do is put very little effort into helping them learn to do so, because it would affect their income.

Looks like a pretty impossible situation now, doesn't it? Next to foster parenting, the government funding goes to the schools. In the era of lack of funding—mostly because of mis-managed health-care dollars over generations and the inability of governments to truly manage health care in any preventable way—this sector takes up a lot of taxpayer dollars. Education is the other sector that is always searching for a bigger piece of the pie. Special-needs children have also brought millions of dollars to the public-education sector, without delivering adequate results for the money. Hope no doubt brought $50,000 in funding to her school, but tell me, why I have seen her improved more in her adult day program in one year than most of her other schooling combined? Especially in the area of communication. Hope was held back communication wise all through her schooling. So much so that she would press her hand against her neck in frustration, leaving a mark. This (I believe) was her way of letting people around her know that she wasn't being heard or listened to. Within several months of being in her adult program, she stopped doing that, and I feel it's because she is around people who care about what she has to communicate.

CHAPTER 16

What about me?

While I was adequately acquainted with moderate self-care before Hope was born, I certainly realized that self-care needed to be high on my priority list. Often times women (especially) put themselves last on their lists. This is backwards, because you have to think about what you're teaching your children by doing that. You're teaching them that you don't matter. This is where respite offered to families is so precious. It's great that families can have help from family, and that is to be expected and normal anyways, but having someone come to your home so you can attend to your needs or the needs of siblings (emotional needs, homework, extra curricular activities, and so on) is a must-have requirement. I started with four hours each week. It rose to twenty-four hours after Andrew was born, and then dropped to fourteen hours each week. A good four of those hours I used just for a yoga class, a facial, manicure, or just a simple walk in nature. I know that families often rally around the family when children are born like this or something unthinkable happens. I just had family support on the one side, and with no sisters and friends who were busy with their own lives, this respite was 100 percent essential.

I had several children's special-services workers. I know some families that still have the same worker after many years. I had many, which meant having to get to know someone else all the time, and having to explain things over and over again. I am not going to lie, carving out time for myself was always easy. It all really came down to values, and if I didn't value myself enough to put myself first, I definitely would not have been able to get through those years, especially the earlier ones, when Hope was little. I worked as flexible of hours as I could, and this allowed me to use more time during the day when the children were in daycare. I would swim three times each week, and start my workday at 10:45 after my morning swim.

CHAPTER 17

For Parents of Special Needs Children and anyone else.

How to cope with grief like this?

When Hope was little, I would often be asked, "How do you remain so strong? How do you cope day to day?" My life became exactly that: day to day. This taught me more about a single moment in time than anything else that I can think of. While I'd had a certain level of self-care ever since I was a teen, I knew I would have to pay extra attention to myself so I would have adequate energy to care for Hope and her big sister. Grieving certainly was a process.

The Process of Grieving

How do you cope with grief like this? That's a big question for many parents of children with disabilities or other medical needs.

The famous "five stages of grief" aren't necessarily predictable when a parent is dealing with a child's loss of health or developmental skills. In the case of developmental skills, you sometimes don't know what is possible, because everyone is different. If you don't try something, that is a sure sign you won't see progress. I decided to expose Hope to everything that her siblings experienced as best she could.

The denial, anger, bargaining, depression, and acceptance may be a whirlwind; one or more stages may pop up unexpectedly when a child misses a milestone altogether or when the parent finds a completely different way of coping and problem-solving.

There is no such thing as a "correct" way to grieve and every situation is different. At one end of the spectrum, a parent may suffer symptoms of Post-Traumatic Stress Disorder, especially after witnessing a child's medical procedures or life-altering events.

When I realized that Hope was developmentally delayed and would not have a typical childhood, I felt a sense of loss on many levels. There were so many unknowns when she was a baby and young child.

Over twenty years later, I still feel sadness or sorrow from time to time. I feel it more for Hope though and only want her happiness. In my heart, I like to feel that she feels good about her life. When the sadness comes, I give myself that time and do something special for myself. Hypnosis and time-line definitely helped me navigate those tricky emotions, and I found myself even healing beyond that, as I became accustomed to this new life. I became much more patient especially with myself and other's.

I made time to explore meditative arts such as yoga, meditations, Tai chi, and explored all sorts of other healing modalities, breathing exercises, positive visualization, and relaxation strategies.

My spirituality grew, as my faith and belief in a higher power and my maternal instinct were all I had some days. I am pleased that I paid close attention to my self-care so that both of those remained strong and clear.

Volunteer work helped me to remove the focus from my family's needs and do something to help others. Generally, the places I would volunteer would be connected to special-needs children, but I did do other charities. It's sometimes easy to get to thinking your problems are the worst, but the truth is that someone else has it worse, so you should do what you can for others. Be kind. It makes you feel better and become a better person.

I researched and advocated for Hope. I was able to discuss her education and therapy with intelligence and clarity and was able to exchange helpful ideas with her team. I was able to implement the results of my research and then see Hope benefit from my efforts. That made me feel really good about making Hope's future better.

I could complain for a really long time about all the lost years of financial deprivation and torture that I've endured, but complaining doesn't change it. I should have never been put in this situation. The people in the hospital are way out of touch with what is out there for biological parents.

Instead, I choose to reflect on what was revealed to me: the hours spent feeding and cuddling a child, knowing full well that her future would be very different from other girls her age. Knowing that I don't regret my losses, because in return I gained something that I had never imagined. I gained a strength that I would never have thought was even possible.

Here are some simple methods of self-care:

- Spend time on a hobby.
- Meet a friend for dinner or coffee.
- Make the beauty of nature part of the day.
- Listen to music.
- Stimulate your intellect.
- Challenge yourself physically.
- Take a dancing class.
- Learn yoga.
- Learn to meditate.
- Indulge in a small treat.
- Plant a garden.
- Get out and meet new people (chances are your friends have abandoned you, because they don't know what to do).

Grief, sorrow, and all types of intense emotion can change anyone, for better or for worse. I know that I am a different person now. I was different when I became a parent. Parenting a child with a disability takes that to a whole new level. People have no idea what this is about until it happens to them or someone they know.

The capacity to grieve is as much a part of us as the capacity to love. Loving was the easiest thing I've ever done. Losing the child I thought I was having was the hardest. Accepting Hope for who she is was the highest form of unconditional love I've ever had before me. When you survive loss, lots of people comment on how strong you are, but no one has the choice to survive the grief they do. It's not an option. You just have to cry in the shower and sob into your pillow and pray you make it. Literally.

I wish I could tell you the pain's not always there. It is, behind every tear and every smile. That's the thing about pain: It demands to be felt. I've learned that, no matter how badly your heart is broken, the world doesn't stop. I just decided to take this challenge and embrace it. It was 100 percent an act of faith. It was about picking up that broken heart, piece by piece, and mending it back together. No one does it for you. It's up to you. You can go around feeling sorry for yourself or you can choose to grow from it. It's that simple.

Who do I see when I look in the miarror? I can honesty say that I see a woman who is purpose and value driven. Rather than seeing the lines and grey hair, I look in her eyes and say, "You've been dealt quite the hand, embraced the journey, and grew into this heartful, wise, and resilient woman, and I am so proud of you!" I see a woman who has been through so much pain and is still standing. I also see a woman who decided not to be defined by her pain, and instead was intent on living a life of joy—a woman who creates her own possibilities.

We all feel better when we have some measure of control over our circumstances. As the parent of a special-needs child, control seems very elusive. Doctors cannot always predict what lies ahead. Different treatments may be attempted until something "works" and your child's condition may change unexpectedly. It will be important to find professionals you can trust to provide two things: professional expertise and care, and recommendations based on the best interests of your child and family. You should also trust your own instincts. Only you know your child best; trust your gut when you sense something is amiss. Then make sure you ask for help. I came across this with Hope. She hasn't been on any medications now for almost ten years. Prior to that, she was put on a mood disorder medication because the doctor was guessing. That neurologist realized she was wrong and ended up discharging Hope from her patient list. Obviously, she realized she had overstepped her boundaries, which affected Hope a great deal and was something she definitely didn't need.

CHAPTER 18

Forgiveness of Self First

It was early in 2002 when I realized that I was at the top of my list of people to make amends to and forgive. Yes, 100 percent me! It had little to do with Hope, per se. It had to do with the situation of my marriage in general at the time she was born and how things went from there. You can only control your side of the situation. I had been the one holding it all together for so long, and letting all that go was an incredible relief. I realized that I had been overly concerned and worried about a man who didn't care two hoots about his health or how his energy affected the home environment. Why I even considered his wishes when he considered no one else's but his own is beyond me. Why do women do this?

I know I was raised in a family where my mom dotted on my dad, and while I didn't do that in my marriage to the same extent, as a family we didn't function well because he didn't want to do anything that was family related. And yet he was the one who had wanted to start a family. I was set up for it, but I didn't sign up for it. I realized before it was too late that I deserved so much better and that, if I didn't do something to make a change, the children's lives would be affected negatively. They would grow up modeling this dysfunction as I did, rather than learning and healing from it. My focus became entirely on myself, striving to be the strongest and best role model for our children. Things are bad enough these days with all the negative topics in the news and the way the environment is treated by corporations at the expense of the people—being positive and taking preventative action doesn't make corporations heaps of money.

Forgiveness of self is the only way you can forgive others, and it's the best feeling to forgive yourself. I meditated a long time about my "amends" list, and realised that my strength from a very young age came from knowing my light! In my life, when I felt darkness closing in, I felt the least amount of strength and had to try the hardest. What I have come to know is this: When I practiced my own program, accepted my own shortcomings and continued to grow from those, my strength always increased and so did my love. When I approached each new situation with the thought "I know nothing," I became the best student, ready and willing to learn all I could. I became a human sponge, leaving the television (nothing on there anyways) and reading a copious number of books on healing and metaphysics. Everything begins with a thought, and my thoughts had to be 100 percent congruent to survive all these changes in my life. It was a good thing I was born an Aries, because taking action is my natural state. Forgiving myself gave me the most energy of all, and after January 2002, a spiritual awakening came on like a strobe light, and it's never turned off.

Psychologists generally define forgiveness as a conscious, deliberate decision to release feelings of resentment or vengeance toward a person or group who has harmed you, regardless of whether they actually deserve your forgiveness.

Forgiveness does not mean forgetting, nor does it mean condoning or excusing offenses. It literally means choosing now to live this way, and I can tell you, real radical forgiveness is the best gift you could ever possibly give to yourself. Be patient with yourself and treat yourself like a newborn baby, feeding yourself good quality food (organic preferably), getting loads of sleep and rest, staying away from or getting rid of vices like smoking and alcohol consumption (too much of anything really), and reading about opening your heart to YOU. That is the foundation of love going outwards, to your children, your spouse or partner, your family, and your community. People need people like you now more than ever. So many are lost, ungrateful for the beautiful earth we all live on and destroying it. Mother earth needs our care and attention so much and the healthier and more aware we all can become the better.

CHAPTER 19

Critical Thinking

Critical thinking is a skill that I learned somewhere, or perhaps it was divine intervention. It could have been somewhere during my schooling years, as I can think of a few teachers that really stood out in a positive way for me. However, looking back, I remember both my parents seeming to struggle with raising three kids, all born between 1962-65. Doesn't that just sound like an impossible task? I parented myself from an early age, and I recall having to figure lots out on my own. Asking why kept me in a solution-based mindset, and I find it rather frustrating when systems just create more problems, swirling in perpetual status quo stagnation.

Here's a simple definition of critical thinking: It's how to logically and rationally think about what's in front of you and getting a true and compete understanding of it. It's the type of thinking that allows you to solve problems easier, just because you are asking the right questions and determining what really matters. Seriously, so many sweat the small stuff, and it's such a waste of time. It accurately acknowledges that the information you need to make any kind of decision will never be 100 percent transparent, and you'll often have to go hunting for it. Therefore, it allows you to bypass your emotional decisions and reasoning, and overall, just think smarter. It can be as simple as asking why several times in a row, when you previously would've only asked once and stayed on the surface (or worse yet, not asked at all). The solution we seek is often not clearly visible, and we might not be even addressing the correct problem. That's what critical thinking helps us with.

Critical thinking is not a matter of accumulating information. A person with a good memory who has recalled a lot of facts is not necessarily a critical thinker. A critical thinker is able to deduce consequences from what he/she knows, and knows how to make use of that information to solve problems. Critical thinking should also not be confused with being argumentative or being critical of other people, because it is not, although it can be used to expose fallacies and bad reasoning.

I always say, "Do you own research." We get thrown copious amounts of information daily, and it can be overwhelming, but if you take matters into your own hands, it can be a very powerful tool. Once I got over the initial emotional upheaval of the worst thing a parent could go through, I became a diligent expert at knowing nothing. This process ensured that I had the mindset to create for Hope the best possible outcome.

When she was born, the professionals at the hospital said, "You know her best," and "There is a lot of help out there." I approached every hurdle with the mindset of "I know nothing." That ensured I'd be open to the process of learning all I could. I'll add a short example from approximately a year after Hope was fitted with a feeding tube. I started just pouring in milk, because she was three and had been eating solid food for a year at this point. The milk went very well, except it wasn't enough calories for her, so the doctor at the feeding clinic suggested switching back to a formula. That went well for about a year, and then she started projectile vomiting the formula. As you can imagine, this was a huge problem.

I recall one time, I had respite to watch her because I had to go out. Just as I was leaving, putting on my shoes, Hope projectile vomited all over me, and even in my purse. I had to completely change and ended up missing my outing, which I had been looking forward to. As this progressed to happening at almost every feed, I was back and forth to the doctor about what to do about this new problem. A drug was prescribed that would empty her stomach quicker. We tried that for a few weeks, but it still happened.

Then a surgery was suggested to make the flap covering the opening to the stomach only go one way. But then I asked, "What if she gets the flu and has to vomit?" That can happen with children or anyone. So, using the critical thinking process described here, I asked the doctor if we could try another formula, as she might just be developing a reaction to the formula. Bingo! That was it and a surgery was averted. Do you think a foster parent would have done the work to advocate? Remember foster parents lose money when the child has fewer medical issues, including being able to walk. The more equipment needed, the more money they get.

I firmly believe that critical thinking is something desperately needed in today's world. No one knows how to think anymore. Sometimes I think the public-school system undid a lot of the good teaching I imparted on my kids (though not so much the eldest, because she was born in 1991). After 2000, the public-school system seemed to take a turn for the worst, and I see more and more parents opting for a private school where real learning with common sense is exercised.

CHAPTER 20

Why?

Why is the system ass backwards? Probably because this way they can extract more funds to build a bigger bureaucracy and fool more people. Why is the government (and I am speaking of our provincial government here in Manitoba) so indignant, saying that they have been there for parents raising special-needs children? They've made a mess with our First Nations families and there are times when I can totally relate. People don't know what they don't know until they find themselves or know someone in the same situation. Things have got to change at a systemic level, because adding more and more layers to a faulty foundation is making it crumble fast. If the system would adopt a more proactive and preventative approach, there would be more resources for other social ills.

This system we have now is, in all ways, really designed to be inadequate until there is a crisis. People laugh until it happens to them. What I've seen over the last twenty plus years is that the only people who seem to benefit are the ones collecting a paycheque to keep this same system. This is human trafficking. The system makes it impossible for biological parents! So much more could be done to give real help to families who face the unfortunate circumstance of having a child born with some sort of abnormality. Let me be clear, I know things have improved since fifty years ago; however, keep in mind that the occurrence of this happening to parents has also increased dramatically.

This circumstance need not ruin lives any more than the grief that a parent must already go through. I can tell you, point blank, that very little is offered in the way of therapy. As a parent, you have to fight for everything, waiting in doctor's offices, and even though it was only with the neurologist, I had a horrible experience with Hope that set her back years. I am grateful that her main doctor didn't make things worse than they had to be. He was really a good doctor, one who listened to what you had to say and followed that guidance. That we worked as a team helped Hope a lot.

If there was one thing that helped me through this pain it was believing in myself. This experience made me stronger than I ever thought I could be. I have felt the fear and held the faith that I could make it, and the only way I did that was by chunking things way down. You have to be easy with yourself. This is more than any one person can handle, so you have to surround yourself with people who care, even if they are hard to find at first. You never know who those people might be. I was surprised by the ones who popped in on me in the hospital. People I hardly saw, maybe once a year, popped in to see us. I sure have been given super-human strength through this, and although it took years for me to write those letters (which I added to this book), there are still more on another computer. It seems like the system is just geared up to break you. Some parents I knew could sue their doctors, as they were insured. Still there's plenty of work to do, but the money isn't an issue, and that is a huge part.

Today, Hope is very happy in her adult day program, but that's the only positive thing in her life. I can see how much happier she is than when she was in school. It seems like her non-verbal communication has increased, and this is because she is being understood in a way that makes her feel validated. Things still aren't great in her living situation, and she spends time living in three homes: her father's, respite, and in mine. I take her out whenever she is with me, or else we spend time sitting in the backyard on the swing, which she enjoys.

I've been working through the system for three years now to find a nice comfortable living situation for Hope and have just been getting the runaround. It's as though such a mess has been made and so many mistakes that they don't know which way is up. Finding her a safe place to live so her siblings can see her has been the hardest, and it's been a series of excuses and manipulation and more excuses. It's very sad when you do the right thing and take responsibility to care for your child, and you're forced to fight for everything including the doctor's appointments. Believe me, many of those appointments are not because the child is sick, but rather because they are tracking, documenting, and learning from the child. Add to all this the momentous task of changing the system for these people, and it's almost like you have to do their job for them. And as if raising children with special needs is not enough work, you are put into the poor house through the process. Part of the proceeds from the sale of this book will go to building a home for Hope to live in, and it will be called Raising Hope.

My Life Now as a Holistic Life Coach

All these events I have been telling you about have led me to where I am today, coaching people like you on exactly what to do to increase confidence, vitality, perseverance, asking, and most of all, self-love, and really step into that feminine power that nobody can take from you. The defining moments in my life, which I detailed in this book, taught me a lot, and I know that I healed through full surrender to my higher power, whom I call God. After that surrender, the universe opened up to me in ways that are surreal to describe. I began to see wonder in *everything*. Taking Hope for walks with Blackie (my black Lab) on those wintery days, where snow would lightly fall, and watching the snowflakes gently fall upon her face and melt, and seeing her expression as they did, brought such joy and wonder to my world. Moments of awe in witnessing a flower coming to full bloom that spring just accentuated my love for plants, which I had felt since my early teens. Now I was intimately watching that unfold. Life is such a gift. I saw little meaning in wasting a moment of it.

WHO ARE MY CLIENTS?

I work with women just like you:

- Investors
- Business Owners
- RealEstate Agents
- Health Professionals
- Psychologists
- Doctors
- Lawyers
- Women who are constantly comparing themselves to others
- Women who are yearning for and intuitively know they need to change
- Women who recognize they MUST initiate CHANGE
- Women who are ready to 100 percent show up for themselves
- Women who are ready to put God first in their life

WHAT TYPE OF PERSONALITY DO I WORK BEST WITH?

I work best with women who are ready to show up!

They don't say...

- If I wasn't in this toxic relationship...
- If I wasn't raised in the family that raised me...
- It's too late for me now; if I wasn't so old...
- I'm not pretty enough
- I'm not skinny enough
- I'm not worth the effort
- God won't approve

INSTEAD, THEY SAY, "ENOUGH IS ENOUGH AND MY TIME IS NOW!"

The journey is winding, and the paths have many twists and turns. Let me save you a lot of grief, if you resonate with anything I've written so far. Society has just begun to step up and take notice of women's contribution to a better world, and WE are growing in numbers, showing up for each other. Men cannot do this for US. It's not that I ignored my situation. I was alone in it and lived to stare the devil down to the ground, to rise up and thrive!

My coaching business specializes in deep inner-healing work, and from this I created my signature empowerment program:

Welcome to YOUR Fabulous Future in 90 Days!!!

Time-Line Therapy: to release the primary emotions of anger, sadness, fear, and guilt, and get the learnings first, so the past is NOT repeated. Release only those emotions that are attached to memories recalled or suppressed.

Hypnosis: To release unwanted habits that were adopted as a result of suppressed emotions that do not serve us well.

Nutritional Council: To get back to REAL nutrition of what the body needs to perform at optimum capacity, given all this newfound energy freed up from the emotional releasing. Customized programs that include treat days that nourish our body and soul at a new level of awareness you may not have realized were possible for you! NEVER DIET AGAIN!

Self Love: Really knowing at a very deep level what is yours and what has been put upon you! This is KEY to wellness.

Spiritual Awareness: Tap into that infinite source of energy that permeates our planet and is waiting patiently for YOU to tap into!

My Signature Program is simple, yet so very EFFECTIVE!

Is this the year when YOU say YES to making the changes that bring YOU to your BEST SELF?

My healings started in getting Reiki treatments in 2001. This immediately tapped me into that infinite source of energy that is always available to us. I attained the Master's training level by 2005. Healing through hypnosis followed, and trainings started in 2005-2011 after performing my practice hours and exams. Talk therapy does help us recognize and sort out the situation we often times find ourselves in; however, it is only through the bodywork and deep healing that we can REALLY HEAL at those deep levels that bring us the FREEDOM and EXPANSION that our souls are starving for. This is REAL TRANSFORMATION.

ARE YOU READY FOR EXPANSION AND FREEDOM?

WHAT WOULD YOUR LIFE LOOK LIKE?

I cleaned up my past and started teaching women FROM VARIOUS WALKS OF LIFE how they can do the same. I watched some improve their lives beyond their expectations! I have since made a commitment to dedicate the rest of my professional life to helping other women be real to themselves and therefore be present to what belongs to them and what doesn't, healing the parts of themselves that have been ignored or forgotten. My ideal client is a professional woman who has put everything on the line to get where she is today and to put her life in its truest perspective so that she can continue to perform to her highest level, while looking after her body mind and spirit and truly serving this planet with integrity, love, and compassion.

Frequently asked Questions:

What makes you different from other "coaches?"

I've been to the burning bush and back! Because of this, I have a unique set of wisdom, insight, and subsequent trainings in various healing modalities that CAN and WILL rebirth your total being to accelerate the infinite flow of love and abundance to you ... be it LOVE, HAPPINESS, and/or MONEY! I was at a level in life where the worst possible thing finally happened before I could see how off the path I was and healed with the help of my higher power. I completely and fully surrendered into that power with my body, mind, and soul before I even knew that training or therapy sessions, other than talk therapy, even existed. I'm also very spiritual, and I don't pretend to hide it either.

What type of personality do you work best with and what is expected of me?

PUT YOUSELF FIRST Holistic Wellness Coaching TM was created for people wanting real change in their lives, who are absolutely excited and very serious about getting results, and are willing to do the work that it takes to make that happen. This means not running around all day long, beating yourself up anymore saying, "I can't do this!" or "It's the way I am!"

Being a woman who's had these life experiences tossed at her and knows the value of healing work, I'm known to work best with other clients in similar situations who want to correct these issues to avoid the disasters in their lives that I had to endure. I have said before that I wish no one would ever go through the pain and suffering that I have experienced as a result of not being true to myself in the first place. YOU are the factor that matters, and life gets real messy real fast when YOU are NOT the FOCUS in YOUR life!

I work with women who are committed to their success no matter what, who are super ready to get going, and just want to know exactly what steps to take to GET THERE and GET VERY CLEAR ON STANDING IN THEIR TRUTH. My clients often tell me, "Just tell me what to do and I'll do it!" Consider what you'll do with me to be a high-octane crash course on every-thing you need to know about releasing the emotions that are driving your behaviors, and adopting a more congruent approach that the universe will respond to with total certainty ... because the universe just opens up and synchronicities are happening. You will be expected to take serious and consistent action (in a loving way of course). No excuses anymore, just a very different way of thinking and full support while you achieve massive changes in your life!

Xoxox

YOU DESERVE IT!!

What exactly is the PUT YOURSELF FIRST HOLISTIC WELLNESS COACHING TM system and what does it include?

PUT YOURSELF FIRST HOLISTIC WELLNESS COACHING TM begins with understanding your true value, where your power really comes from, how to manifest what you want (including more $$$$$$$ money), and creating powerful intentions that get you results!

My Signature Program Consists of twelve modules over ninety days

Set your intentions: Week 1

We get crystal clear on what you want to experience in your personnel life and/or business. You'll learn the difference between setting goals and setting intentions. Before you can manifest what you want, you have to know what you want.

Release your inner resistance: Week 2-5

You may intellectually know what you need to do to make these changes but are still struggling with procrastination, feeling stuck, and spinning in circles. You'll be learning proven techniques to release the primary emotions that cause these behaviors in the first place. Depending on how many primary emotions are driving your behaviors, this could take several weeks as we release them one at a time. RELEASE them for good!

Releasing Unwanted Habits: Week 3-5

Healthier relationships, healthier eating habits, excessive alcohol consumption, smoking, inactivity, overactivity, food addictions, shopping addictions... Permitting your body—that vehicle of awareness—to be nourished from the inside out. Greater spiritual awareness involves synchronicities and opportunities. The law of attraction will start to really work for you now!

Focus and Dial It In: Week 6

Now that you are feeling much lighter and brighter, shedding away years or even decades of self-defeating behaviors that kept you in a victim mentality, you are starting to feel the "balance" permeate your entire being, now filling your days with greater awareness and energy. Are there any adjustments that you'd like to make with your intentions? Often as we become more aware, more balanced within ourselves, our original intentions change a bit. Are there any changes you want to make?

Nourishing with Nutrients: Week 7-9

This week starts with a food and herb cleanse that resets your body's addiction to sugar. This is a common issue for everyone in the western world. I can recommend what I know is the best on the market today and easiest to follow.

Women's bodies are meant to be nourished, and together we explore how a woman's body works for optimal performance. Now that the baggage from your past has been successfully cleared through time-line therapy, you are craving nutritious foods. You will learn about daily cleansing and re-adjusting, including making meal plans that work. Foods that nourish become pleasurable because you now LOVE yourself fully and completely. This opens you up to even greater universal energies that have been here and available to you.

Exploring and Embracing Your New Life: 9-12

Time to celebrate! We will focus a lot of our time really celebrating your new accomplishments. Your now healthy confidence is sky rocketing, and you consistently produce greater and greater results! It is important that you celebrate what shows up, so that you can pave the way for even more success!

Examples of benefits in working with PUT YOURSELF FIRST Holistic Wellness Coaching:

- Let go and release trauma in the body
- Forgive self, God, and others, and therefore find more peace and compassion
- Anxiety dissipates so peace and calm can set in
- Create new standards and nurture yourself
- Fill your tank first!
- Feel empowered and excited about the future
- Fall back in love with yourself ... your life started this way
- More creative, more ease, more grace in your life
- Vibrate as a longing being to become truly unconditionally loving with all your relationships
- Develop more compassion for yourself and others
- Learn how to say NO ... plus honoring your "yes's" and "no's"
- Connect with your intuition
- Open your heart and expand into your true being
- Rewrite your story by cleaning up your past
- End the drama cycles and patterns
- Raise your self-esteem and self-confidence to epic levels
- Release habits that no longer serve your highest purpose in life
- Create new beliefs and healthy habits that nurture your body, mind, and spirit.
- Be clear, honest, and concise in your communication.
- Create healthy boundaries
- Gain unshakeable confidence in yourself
- Understand how your soul is awakening and developing.
- Learn proven techniques for releasing your internal resistance and self-sabotaging tendencies, so that you can take action and start living your purpose and passion with ease.

Can I contact some of your former clients to see what it's like to work with you?

Yes, I encourage you to! Please go to the Client Testimonials page (http://bit.ly/2SFoUVH). See which ones you feel drawn to, either because the person has gotten the results you want to get too, or perhaps because that person is in a similar situation. Then feel free to email or call them and ask what they got from working with me and my programs.

How quickly can I expect results?

That depends on how quickly you can make those inner shifts. Some clients are ready to go and clear out the past and take action to secure a desired outcome in a very short time frame. This all depends on how quickly you can let go of emotions. Remember, it is key to get the learnings before an emotion is released, and I guide you to find that first before the emotion is released.

Okay, I'm ready to do this for myself, but I have a couple of additional questions. Can I call you?

Good. Sounds like you're ready to be pulled into your future! Yes, if you have a couple of questions, just email me at KIMPARKE123@SHAW.CA or kimparke321@gmail.com or call directly 204-899-0719, OR MESSAGE ME ON FACEBOOK. I USUALLY RESPOND WITHIN 24 HOURS DURING THE WEEK! And I'll be happy to walk you through the different options to see which one will be the very best for you. I can't wait to see you succeed and am honored to be the one to help you.

SOME LAST WORDS...

As 2019 is here, I want you to choose what and why this year will be like no other year yet!

While I am a kind woman who cares about people, I don't work with everyone who contacts me. I only work with women who are ready and willing to INVEST in themselves and better their lives for themselves first, which benefits everyone around them.

You have a purpose while you are here: to share your gifts with this world. You are a divine being of light and deserve to prosper and use those funds to explore this beautiful planet.

To show up and embrace your authenticity every day and watch your world shift into magic!

ABOUT THE AUTHOR

Kim Parke has taken on countless professional positions over the years, in her efforts to support her family while juggling the time constraints of raising a child with special needs on her own. Most recently, she has created a Ninety-Day Holistic Wellness Coaching Program for anyone who wants to create real and lasting change in their life, using her life experiences and knowledge to help others in need. Paired with the proceeds from this book—which she hopes will shed some light on our government's need for systemic change, in terms of how biological families of disabled children are treated—she hopes to eventually build a specialized home for Hope, where she can be supported and happy and no longer victimized by a system that just covers the bare minimum of care.

Born and raised in Winnipeg, Kim lives with her nineteen-year-old son, and sees Hope every chance she gets.

CPSIA information can be obtained
at www.ICGtesting.com
Printed in the USA
LVHW010230111219
639964LV00002B/2/P